Renal Diet Cookbook for Beginners

The Proven Method That Will Help You Keep Your CKD Under Control By Reducing Your Kidney's Workload. Enjoy Many Delicious And Easy Recipes Low In Sodium, Potassium, And Phosphorus. Suitable For The Whole Family

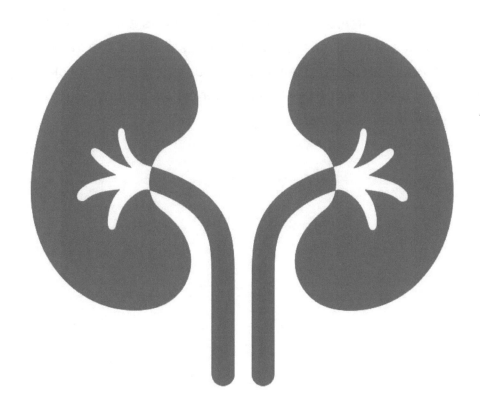

Samantha Smith

Contents

· ·

Introduction   5

Dietary Recommendations   7

   1.1 Sodium   7

   1.2 Potassium   8

   1.3 Phosphorus   9

   1.4 Proteins   10

   1.5 Fluids   10

Food Items Ideal for Renal Diet   13

Renal-Friendly Breakfast Options   19

Renal-Friendly Desserts Options   27

Renal-Friendly Snacks   35

Salad Options   44

Vegetable Recipes   51

Fish And Seafood Recipes   59

Renal-Friendly Meat Options   67

28 Days Meal Plan   81

Conclusion   92

Recipes Index   93

Introduction

Eating properly is essential to your therapy and may improve your mood. A new diet is an important component of your recovery. It will not only make you feel better, but it will also help you prevent problems associated with your renal illness, such as fluid retention. Overload and excessive blood potassium, bone damage, and weight loss are all symptoms of renal problems. As your kidney function is critical for eliminating food waste, it is important to note that every person will have different requirements from their diet. The kidneys excrete urea, a dietary protein, salt, potassium, and other minerals. If the kidney function is hindered, these chemicals may accumulate in the body.

A rigorous diet may help to reduce this buildup and its consequences. A low-sodium, low-phosphorus, and low-potassium diet is known as a renal diet. The necessity of consuming a protein-based diet and conserving fluids is stressed on a renal diet. Potassium and calcium limitations may be necessary for certain people. As each person is different, a dietician may work with each patient to create a renal diet tailored to their particular needs. It is important to eat well to maintain your renal health. Phosphorus, potassium, and sodium must all be limited in people with a renal illness. A renal diet is sometimes referred to as a dialysis diet or a kidney diet. Blood waste is produced as a result of food and beverage consumption. People with kidney disease must adopt a renal diet to decrease the waste in their tissues. You must keep track of everything you drink and eat if you have chronic kidney disease (CKD). This is because your kidneys aren't as effective as they should be in removing waste from your body. As a result, a kidney-friendly diet may help you stay healthy for extended periods. It is possible that adopting a renal diet may improve kidney efficiency and postpone kidney failure. The traditional renal diet is the best diet for those with kidney disease.

Dietary adjustments, including restrictions, are implemented only as needed and are tailored to the individual's age, food requirements, and development. Your calories, protein, fat, phosphorus, salt, calcium, potassium, and hydration consumption may need to be changed. Limitations are maintained as flexible as possible to help satisfy energy needs and encourage adherence. The restrictions may be raised or decreased depending on your response to the changes. In the case of a child's nutritional status, age, development, anthropometrics, eating habits, residual renal activity, biochemistry, renal replacement therapy, medicines, and psychological state, treatment via diet requires regular monitoring and adjustments. Your health is influenced by what you eat and drink. Eating a balanced, low-fat, low-salt diet will assist you in maintaining a healthy weight and controlling your blood pressure. If you have diabetes, carefully selecting what you drink and eat may help you manage your blood pressure. Controlling blood sugar and blood pressure may help prevent kidney disease from progressing. This book contains a wealth of information on a kidney-friendly renal diet and delicious kidney-friendly recipes.

Dietary Recommendations

· ·

A kidney-friendly diet is a way of eating that prevents additional kidney damage. Because certain minerals and fluids, such as electrolytes, do not accumulate in the body, you must avoid certain foods and drinks. You must ensure that you consume adequate Proteins, vitamins, calories, and minerals. A kidney-friendly diet may help prevent additional damage to your kidneys. A kidney-friendly diet restricts certain foods to prevent minerals from building up in your body. A renal diet may enhance kidney function and delay the development of complete kidney failure. This diet aims to maintain your electrolyte, mineral, and fluid levels control while you're on dialysis for CKD. Dialysis patients must follow this diet to avoid waste accumulation in the body. A renal diet is a low-Sodium, low-phosphorus, and low-Proteins diet. A renal diet stresses the necessity of eating high-quality Proteins and, in most cases, reducing fluid intake. Some individuals may additionally need potassium and calcium restrictions. Because every person's body is different, each patient must engage with a renal nutritionist to develop a diet that's customized to their specific requirements.

The following are some substances to keep an eye on to support a renal diet:

● 1.1 Sodium

Sodium is an element that is found in almost all-natural foods. The terms "salt" and "Sodium" are often used interchangeably. Salt, on the other hand, is a Sodium-chloride compound. Salt or Sodium in various forms may be present in our foods. Because of the additional salt, processed foods typically have greater Sodium levels. One of the body's three basic electrolytes is Sodium (potassium and chloride are the other two). Electrolytes regulate the flow of fluids into or out of the tissues and cells of the body.

The function of Sodium is involved in the following processes:

1. Heart rate and blood volume control
2. Nerve functioning and muscle contraction are both regulated.
3. Keeping the blood's acid-base balance in check
4. Keeping a balance between how much liquid the body retains and how much it excretes

Why should renal patients keep a close eye on their salt intake?

For individuals with renal illness, too much salt may be hazardous because their kidneys cannot properly remove additional Sodium and fluid from the body. The accumulation of salt and fluid in the tissues and circulation may lead to:

1. Increased thirst
2. Inflammation in the legs, hands, and face is known as edema.
3. Blood pressure that is too high,
4. Excess fluid in the circulation may cause your heart to overwork, causing it to become enlarged and feeble.
5. Shortness of breath: fluid may accumulate in the lungs, making breathing harder.

How can patients keep track of their salt consumption?

Always read the labels on foods. The amount of Sodium in a product is always stated. Keep an eye on the serving portions. Use fresh meats instead of using processed meats. Fresh fruits and vegetables, as well as no-salt-added frozen foods, are good choices. Avoid processed foods as much as possible. Compare brands and choose the lowest Sodium options. Use spices that don't include "salt" in their name (choose garlic powder instead of garlic salt.) When cooking at home, leave out the salt. Limit salt intake to 400 milligrams each meal and 150 milligrams every Snack.

● *1.2 Potassium*

Potassium is a mineral that may be found in a variety of foods as well as in the human body. Potassium levels in adults typically range from 3.5 to 5.0 mill moles per liter.

The function of potassium: Potassium helps maintain the heartbeat and the muscles in good functioning order. Potassium is also required to maintain the bloodstream's fluid and electrolyte balance. The kidneys aid in maintaining a healthy potassium balance in the body by excreting excess potassium into the urine.

Why is it important for renal patients to keep track of their potassium intake?

When the kidneys are damaged, the body's potassium levels rise because the kidneys cannot eliminate extra potassium. Hyperkalemia is a condition in which there is too much potassium in the blood, which may lead to:

1. Muscle deterioration
2. An erratic heartbeat
3. slow heartbeat
4. Attacks on the heart
5. Death

How can patients keep track of their potassium consumption?

When the kidneys no longer control potassium, the quantity of potassium that enters the body must be monitored. Potassium can be monitored in many ways, which are the following:

1. Make an eating plan with the help of a renal dietitian.
1. Potassium-rich foods should be avoided.
2. Limit yourself to 8 ounces of dairy products each day. Fresh fruits and vegetables are the best options.
3. Avoid Potassium-containing salt replacements and spices.
4. Avoid potassium chloride by reading the labels on packaged goods.
5. Keep an eye on the serving size. Keeping a food diary is a good idea.

● 1.3 Phosphorus

Phosphorus is an important mineral for bone health and growth.

The function of phosphorus: Phosphorus is also important for forming structural tissue and organs and moving muscles. When Phosphorus-rich food is eaten and digested, the Phosphorus is absorbed by the small intestines and deposited in the bones.

Why is it important for renal patients to keep track of their Phosphorus: intake?

Normal functioning kidneys may remove surplus Phosphorus in your bloodstream. When kidney function is impaired, the kidneys cannot eliminate excess Phosphorus from the body. High Phosphorus levels may deplete calcium in your bones, causing them to become brittle. Calcium deposits in the eyes, blood vessels, airways, and heart are also risky.

How can patients keep track of their Phosphorus consumption?

Phosphorus is present in a variety of foods. As a result, individuals with impaired kidney function should see a renal dietician control their Phosphorus levels. Here are some tips for keeping Phosphorus levels in check:

1. Learn which foods have reduced Phosphorus content.
1. Keep a careful eye on the serving size. At meals and Snacks, consume smaller amounts of high-Proteins foods. Consume fresh fruit and vegetable.
2. Consult your doctor regarding the use of phosphate binders at mealtime.
3. Avoid buying and using Phosphorus-fortified packaged foods.
4. On ingredient labels, look for Phosphorus or phrases that start with the letter "PHOS."
5. Keep a dietary diary.

● 1.4 *Proteins*

Proteins are huge, complex molecules that perform several important functions in the human body.

The function of Proteins: They are essential for the construction, function, and control of the body's tissues and organs, and they perform most of their activity in cells.

Why is it important for renal patients to keep track of their Protein intake?

Proteins are not an issue for kidneys that are in good shape. Proteins are normally eaten, and wastage products are produced and filtered by the kidney's nephrons. The waste is then converted to urine with extra renal Proteins. On the other hand, damaged kidneys fail to eliminate Protein waste, which builds up in the blood.

How can patients keep track of their Protein consumption?

Calculating Proteins intake is difficult for Chronic Kidney Illness patients since the quantity varies depending on the stage of the disease. Proteins are necessary for tissue development and other physiological functions; therefore, follow your nephrologist's or renal dietician's recommendations for your particular stage of illness.

● 1.5 *Fluids*

Water makes up most of the human body, accounting for about 60% of total body weight. The quantity of fluid in the blood varies somewhat depending on the individual's gender, age, and hydration state. As the average proportion of water in human blood is about 60%, the number may range between approximately 45 and 75%.

Functions: The fluid acts as a protective and cushioning agent for joints and organs. Avoid dehydration by drinking enough water. Headaches, tiredness, disorientation, and irritability are all symptoms of dehydration. Fluid aids in urine production and removes waste products from the body via the kidneys. The fluid keeps the urinary system healthy, which helps to avoid infections. Fluid aids in the regulation of body temperature. Elderly individuals can get hot and ill if they do not drink enough liquids. Fluid aids in the digestion (breakdown) of food. The fluid keeps feces smooth and regular, which helps to avoid constipation. Fluid is an essential component of blood since it aids in the transport of nutrients throughout the body.

Why is it important for renal patients to keep track of their Fluid intake?

Fluid management is critical for patients with Chronic Kidney Disease in the latter stages since normal fluid intake may lead to fluid buildup in the body, which can be hazardous. Because dialysis patients' urine production is frequently reduced, fluid buildup in the body may strain the heart and lungs undue.

How can patients keep track of their Fluids consumption?

The fluid allowance for each patient is determined individually, based on urine production and dialysis settings. It's critical to stick to your nephrologist's/fluid nutritionist's consumption recommendations. To keep their fluid consumption under control, patients should:

1. Drink just as much as your doctor prescribes.
2. Keep track of the number of liquids you use while cooking.

Food Items Ideal for Renal Diet

Researchers are discovering more and more links between chronic diseases, inflammation, and "superfoods" that may decrease or protect against harmful Fatsty acid oxidation, which occurs when oxygen in your system interacts with lipids in your blood and cells, resulting in detrimental Fatsty acid oxidation. Excessive oxidation of lipids and cholesterol generates molecules known as free radicals, which may damage your Proteins, cell membranes, and DNA. Heart disease, cancer, Alzheimer's disease, Parkinson's disease, and other chronic and degenerative illnesses have been linked to oxidative damage. Conversely, antioxidant-rich foods may aid in neutralizing free radicals and the body's protection. The renal diet has several anti-oxidant foods, making it an excellent choice for dialysis users or those with chronic kidney disease (CKD). Because people with kidney illness have more inflammation and are more likely to develop cardiovascular disease, lifestyle changes, including consuming healthy meals, engaging with a renal nutritionist, and following a renal diet of kidney-friendly foods, are critical. The following are some foods that are great for a kidney-friendly diet. Talk to your renal dietitian if you want to include these leading kidney-friendly items in your healthy eating plan.

Recall that these meals are suitable for everyone, including family members and friends who do not have a renal illness or are not on dialysis. Keeping your kitchen stocked with delicious, healthy, kidney-friendly meals is a big part of sticking to your renal diet.

Here are 20 of the greatest meals for renal disease sufferers.

1. **CAULIFLOWER:** Cauliflower is a healthy vegetable high in vitamin C, vitamin K, and B folate, among other nutrients. It also includes inflammatory chemicals such as the phenol family and is high in fiber. In addition, potatoes substitution uses mashed cauliflower for a low potassium side dish.

1 cup (124 grams) cooked cauliflower contains: 19 mg Sodium, 176 mg potassium, 40 mg Phosphorus

2. **BLUEBERRIES** are high in minerals and antioxidants, making them one of the healthiest foods you can consume. These delicious berries, in particular, are full of antioxidants called anthocyanins, which may defend against heart disease, cancer, cognitive decline, and diabetes. They're also low in salt, Phosphorus, and potassium, making them a great complement to a kidney-friendly diet.

One cup (148 grams) of fresh blueberries contains: 1.5 mg Sodium, 114 mg potassium, 18 mg Phosphorus

3. **STRIPED BASS:** Sea bass is a high-quality Proteins rich in omega-3 Fatty acids, which are very beneficial Fats. Omega-3 Fatty acids are anti-inflammatory and may lower the risk of cognitive impairment, melancholy, and anxiety. Sea bass has lower Phosphorus: content than other seafood, even though all fish are rich in Phosphorus: To maintain your Phosphorus: level control, you should eat modest amounts.

Cooked sea bass, three ounces (85 grams), contains: 74 mg Sodium, 279 mg potassium, 211 mg Phosphorus

4. **GRAPES (RED):** Red grapes are tasty and pack a lot of nutrients into a tiny package. They're rich in vitamin C and flavonoids, antioxidants that have been proven to decrease inflammation. Red grapes are also rich in resveratrol, a flavonoid proven to improve heart health, protect against diabetes, and slow cognitive decline.

These delicious fruits are good for your kidneys since a half-cup (75 grams) of them contains:1.5 mg Sodium:, 144 mg potassium, 15 mg Phosphorus

5. **WHITES OF EGGS:** Although egg yolks are nutritious, they are rich in Phosphorus: making egg whites a preferable option for people on a renal diet. Egg whites are a good source of Proteins that is easy on the kidneys. They're also a great option for dialysis patients who require a lot of Proteins but have to watch their Phosphorus: intake.

Two big egg whites (66 grams) contain 110 mg Sodium, 108 mg potassium, 10 mg Phosphorus

6. **GARLIC:** The quantity of Sodium: in a person's diet, including additional salt, should be limited if they have renal issues. Garlic is a tasty salt substitute that adds flavor to meals and offers nutritional advantages. It includes sulfur compounds with anti-inflammatory effects and is a rich source of manganese, vitamin C, and vitamin B6.

Three garlic cloves (9 grams) contain: 1.5 mg Sodium, 36 mg potassium, 14 mg Phosphorus

7. **BUCKWHEAT:** Although many whole grains are rich in Phosphorus: buckwheat is an exception. Buckwheat is a nutrient-dense grain rich in B vitamins, magnesium, iron, and fiber. Buck-

wheat is also gluten-free, making it an excellent option for celiac disease or gluten sensitivity sufferers.

A half-cup (84 grams) of cooked buckwheat contains: 3.5 mg Sodium, 74 mg potassium, phosphorus (mg): 59

8. **EXTRA VIRGIN OLIVE OIL:** Olive oil is a good source of Fats and low in Phosphorus: so it's a good choice for renal problems. People with a severe renal illness often struggle to maintain weight, making nutritious, high-calorie meals like olive oil essential. The bulk of the Fats in olive oil is oleic acid, a monounsaturated Fats with anti-inflammatory effects. Furthermore, since monounsaturated Fats are stable at high temperatures, olive oil is a healthy cooking option.

One tablespoon (13.5 grams) of olive oil contains: 0.3 mg Sodium, 0.1 mg potassium, phosphoros (mg): 0

9. **CABBAGE:** Cabbage is a member of the cruciferous vegetable family, which means it's high in vitamins, minerals, and plant compounds. It's high in vitamin K, vitamin C, and a variety of B vitamins. It also contains insoluble fiber, which maintains your digestive system healthy by encouraging regular bowel movements and providing weight to your stool.

Plus, one cup (70 grams) of shredded cabbage contains: 13 mg Sodium:, 119 mg potassium, 18 mg Phosphorus

10. Chicken without the skin Although some individuals with renal problems need to restrict their Proteins consumption, supplying the body with a sufficient quantity of high-quality Proteins is essential for good health. Phosphorus, potassium, and Sodium: are lower in skinless chicken breasts than in skin-on chicken. Choose fresh chicken instead of pre-made roasted chicken when purchasing chicken since it includes a lot of salt and Phosphorus.

three ounces (84 grams) of skinless chicken breast 63 mg Sodium, 216 mg potassium, phosphorus (mg): 192

11. **BELL PEPPERS:** Bell peppers include a lot of minerals, but they're less potassium than other vegetables. These vibrantly colored peppers are high in vitamin C, a strong antioxidant. One small red bell pepper (74 grams) provides 105 percent of the daily vitamin C requirement. They're also high in vitamin A, an essential component for immunological function, frequently hampered by kidney illness.

One small red pepper (74 grams) contains: 3 mg Sodium, 156 mg potassium, 19 mg Phosphorus

12. Onions: Onions are a great way to flavor renal-diet meals without adding salt. It may be difficult to cut down on salt, but delicious salt substitutes are essential. When onions are sautéed with garlic and olive oil, they provide flavor to meals without jeopardizing kidney health. Furthermore, onions are rich in vitamin C, manganese, and B and prebiotic fibers, which feed good gut flora and help keep your digestive tract healthy.

One tiny onion (70 grams) contains: 3 mg Sodium, 102 mg potassium, 20 mg Phosphorus

13. Arugula: Potassium-rich greens like spinach and kale are difficult to include in a renal diet. On the other hand, Arugula is a nutrient-dense green with low potassium content, making it an excellent option for kidney-friendly salads and side dishes. Arugula is high in vitamin K and the minerals manganese and calcium, which are both beneficial to bone health. This healthy green also includes nitrates, proven to help those with kidney diseases by reducing blood pressure.

A cup of raw Arugula (20 grams) contains: 6 mg Sodium, 74 mg potassium, 10 mg Phosphorus

14. Macadamia nuts: Nuts are rich in Phosphorus and should be evaded by individuals on a renal diet. Macadamia nuts, on the other hand, are a wonderful choice for individuals with renal issues. They contain considerably less Phosphorus: than common nuts such as peanuts and almonds. They're also high in healthy Fats, B vitamins, magnesium, copper, iron, and manganese, among other minerals.

One ounce (28 grams) of macadamia nuts contains: 1.4 mg Sodium, 103 mg potassium, 53 mg Phosphorus

15. Radish: Radishes are crisp vegetables that may be used in a renal diet. This is because they are poor in potassium and Phosphorus: but rich in other essential minerals. Radishes are high. Vitamin C is an antioxidant linked to a lower risk of heart disease and cataracts. In addition, their peppery flavor enhances the flavor of low-Sodium: meals.

A half-cup (58 grams) of sliced radishes contains: 23 mg Sodium, 135 mg potassium, 12 mg Phosphorus

16. Turnips; Turnips are renal-friendly, and they're a great replacement for potassium-rich foods like winter squash and potatoes. Fiber and vitamin C abound in these root veggies. They're also a good source of manganese and vitamin B6. They may be roasted or cooked and mashed to provide a nutritious side dish for a renal diet.

A half-cup (78 grams) of cooked turnips contains: 12.5 mg Sodium, 138 mg potassium, 20 mg Phosphorus

17. Pineapple: Potassium is abundant in tropical fruits such as oranges, bananas, and kiwis. Pineapple, fortunately, is a delicious, low-potassium option for people with renal issues. Pineapple is also high in fiber, manganese, vitamin C, and bromelain, an anti-inflammatory enzyme.

One cup (165 grams) of pineapple chunks contains: 2 milligrams of Sodium, 180 mg potassium, 13 mg Phosphorus

18. Cranberries: Cranberries are good for the urinary system and the kidneys. A-type proanthocyanins are phytonutrients that inhibit bacteria from adhering to the urinary system and bladder lining, preventing infection. This is especially beneficial for individuals with renal illness since they are more susceptible to urinary infections. Cranberries may be consumed fresh, dried, cooked, or as a juice. Potassium, Phosphorus, and Sodium: levels are all extremely low.

One cup (100 grams) of fresh cranberries contains: 2 milligrams of Sodium, 80 mg potassium, 11 mg Phosphorus

19. Shiitake mushrooms: Shiitake mushrooms are a delicious item that may be considered as a plant-based meat replacement for people on a renal diet who need to keep their Proteins intake low. Copper, vitamin B, manganese, and selenium are all abundant. They also include a significant quantity of plant-based Proteins and nutritional fiber. Shiitake mushrooms have less potassium than portabella mushrooms and white button mushrooms, so they're a good option for those on a diet plan.

1 cup (145 grams) cooked shiitake mushroom contains: 6 mg Sodium, 170 mg potassium, 42 mg Phosphorus

20. Bulgur: Bulgur is a whole grain wheat product that is a great kidney-friendly alternative to other high-Phosphorus, high-potassium whole grains. Iron, vitamins B and magnesium are all plentiful in this healthy grain. It's also high in plant-based Proteins and dietary fiber, which benefit digestive health.

A half-cup (91-gram) portion of bulgur contains 4.5 mg Sodium, 62 mg potassium 36 mg Phosphorus.

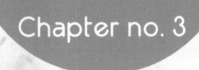

Chapter no. 3

Renal-Friendly Breakfast Options

• •

Do you ever go without Breakfast because you don't have enough time? We're here to help you out! Thanks to everything from bagels to eggs, the most important foods become the easiest meals of the day. You may have delicious prepared quick **Breakfast** dishes while following the Kidney diet plan. A list of several of them is provided below. One of these easy **Breakfast** dishes is worth a shot. So, what are you waiting for? Gather the materials and prepare one of these quick kidney-friendly meals to satiate your appetite.

1. Fluffy Homemade Buttermilk Pancakes

 Servings: 9 (1 serving is equal to 2 4-inch pancakes)

 Preparation Time: 5 minutes

 Cooking Time: 15 minutes

Ingredients:

- » 2 cups of all-purpose flour
- » ¼ cup of canola oil and
- » 1 tablespoon canola oil (needed for cooking)
- » 1 and a half teaspoons of baking soda
- » 1 teaspoon cream of tartar
- » 2 cups of low-Fats buttermilk
- » 2 large eggs, beaten
- » 2 tablespoons of sugar

Directions:

- » Melt the butter in a pan over medium heat.
- » Combine the dry Ingredients: in a large mixing bowl. In a mixing bowl, combine the dry Ingredients: with the oil, buttermilk, and egg. With a mixer or a spoon, combine all until they are completely moistened.
- » Use a tablespoon of canola oil to grease the pan. Using a 1/3-cup measuring cup, scoop the pancake batter onto the griddle. Each pancake should have a diameter of around 4 inches. Allow around 2" space between the pancakes for easy flipping. Flip your pancakes with a spatula when the bubbles on the top have almost vanished. Allow the second side to brown until the center no longer seems wet.
- » Place on a serving platter.
- » For a nutritious twist, serve with fresh berries and a side of eggs.

- » *Tip:* Freeze any leftover buttermilk pancakes and reheat as needed for a quick Breakfast.

Nutrients per Serving: Calories: 175, Fat: 7.2g, Carbohydrates: 22g, Proteins: 5g, Sodium: 402 mg, Phosphorus: 28 mg, Potassium: 170mg

2. Stuffed Breakfast Biscuits

· · · · · · · · · · · · · · · · · ·

 Servings: 12 (1 serving = 1 biscuit)

 Preparation Time: 10 minutes

 Cooking Time: 20 minutes

Ingredients:

» 2 cups of flour
» 1 tablespoon of lemon juice
» ¾ cup of milk
» 1 tablespoon of sugar (can be replaced with honey)
» ½ teaspoon of baking soda
» 8 tablespoons of softened unsalted butter, softened
» 4 eggs, beaten lightly
» 8 ounces or 1¼ chopped of reduced-Sodium bacon
» 1 cup of Cheddar cheese, required in shredded form
» ¼ cup of scallions, thinly chopped

Directions:

» Make scrambled eggs and keep it slightly underdone.
» Cook the bacon until it's nice and crispy.
» Combine all four Ingredients: in a mixing bowl and put them aside.
» Combine all dry Ingredients: in a large mixing dish or plate.
» Cut in unsalted butter with a fork or pastry until pea-size or smaller.
» Make a well in the middle of the mixture and knead the milk and lemon juice.
» Use a muffin pan liner or gently oil and flour the bottom and sides of the muffin tins.
» Fill muffin pans with 14 cups of batter.
» Preheat the oven to 425°F and bake for 10-12 minutes until golden brown.

» *Tip:* For a quick Breakfast, freeze the leftover biscuits.

Nutrients per Serving: Calories: 330, Fat: 23g, Carbohydrates: 19g, Proteins: 11g, Sodium: 329 mg, Phosphorus: 170 mg, Potassium: 168.

3. Oatmeal with Honey and Fruit

 Serving: 1

 Preparation Time: 20 minutes

 Cooking Time: 20 minutes

Ingredients:

» 1/2 cup of oats
» 1 cup of water
» 1 teaspoon of honey
» Low-potassium fruit (like apples or pears)

Directions:

» Combine the oats and water in a pot, then heat until boiling.
» Lower the heat and let it simmer for about 10-15 minutes. Stir every now and then until the oats are soft and have absorbed the water.
» Take the pot off the heat and mix in the honey.
» Pour the oatmeal into a bowl, top with your chosen fruit cut into pieces, and it's ready to serve!

Nutritional value: Calories: 200, Fat: 4, Carbohydrates: 40g, Proteins: 6g, Sodium: 15mg, Phosphorus: 130mg, Potassium 170mg

4. Loaded Veggie Eggs

 Servings: 2

 Preparation Time: 5 minutes

 Cooking Time: 12 – 15 minutes

Ingredients:

» 2 whole eggs, beaten
» 1 garlic clove, finely chopped
» 1 cup of cauliflower
» 3 cups of fresh spinach
» 1/4 teaspoon of black pepper
» 1/4 cup of bell pepper, chopped
» 1/4 cup of onion, chopped finely
» 1 tablespoon of oil of choice (coconut or avocado oil is good for high heat)
» Fresh parsley and spring onion for garnish

Directions:

» Whisk together the eggs and peppers until smooth, then put aside.
» In a large skillet, heat the oil over medium heat.
» In a pan, sauté the onions and peppers until the peppers are transparent and golden.
» Add the garlic and stir briefly to mix before adding the cauliflower and spinach.
» Sauté veggies for 5 minutes, then reduce heat to medium-low.
» Add the eggs and mix them in with the veggies.
» Garnish with chopped basil or spring onions after the eggs are fully cooked. If you don't have a potassium limitation, serve with a side of vibrant, fresh tomatoes sprinkled with cracked black pepper. With these, a little cheddar or a strong, sharp cheese would be great.

Nutrients per Serving: Calories: 240, Fat: 16.6g, Carbohydrates: 7.8g, Proteins: 15.3, Sodium: 150mg, Phosphorus: 150 mg, Potassium 750m

5. Super Simple Baked Pancake

 Serving: 1 wedge or 1/4 recipe

 Preparation Time: 10 minutes

 Cooking Time: 45 minutes

Ingredients::

» 1/8 teaspoon of nutmeg
» 1/2 cup of milk
» 1/2 cup all-purpose white flour
» 1/4 teaspoon salt
» 1 egg, beaten
» 1 tablespoon of vegetable oil

Directions::

» Preheat the oven to 450 degrees Fahrenheit.
» In a medium mixing bowl or deep dish, beat the egg and milk together using a wire whisk or an electric mixer.
» Blend in the flour, salt, and nutmeg until well combined (small lumps of flour left in the batter are okay).
» Pour vegetable oil into a 9" oven-safe skillet or pie pan and heat for 5 minutes in a preheated oven.
» Pour batter into the pan carefully and bake for 18 to 20 minutes, uncovered. (Do not open the oven door until the pancake has swelled up and become crisp around the edges.) When cooked, the middle will be nicely browned).
» Cut into four wedges and serve with pancake syrup or fruity spread.

» *Tip:* Nondairy alternatives, such as rice milk or nondairy creamer, may be used instead of milk. Potassium and Phosphorus levels will be somewhat lower. Add one extra egg white for additional Proteins.

Nutrients per Serving: Calories: 189, Fat: 5g, Carbohydrates: 27g, Proteins: 8g, Sodium: 300mg, Phosphorus: 135mg, Potassium 80mg.

6. Egg and Sausage Breakfast Sandwich

 Serving: 1

 Preparation Time: 5 minutes

 Cooking Time: 5 – 10 minutes

Ingredients::

» Nonstick cooking spray
» 1 English muffin
» 1 tablespoon shredded natural sharp cheddar cheese
» 1/4 cup of liquid low-cholesterol egg replacement
» 1 turkey sausage patty

Directions::

» Pour the egg product into a small pan with nonstick cooking spray and cook over moderate heat. When the egg is nearly done, flip it over with a spatula and cook for another 30 seconds.
» Toast English Muffins for usage.
» Place the turkey sausages patty on a dish, cover with a clean paper towel, and heat for 1 minute or until done according to package directions.
» Assemble an English muffin with a cooked egg (fold to fit the muffin). Top with a sausage patty, sharp cheddar cheese, and the other half of the muffin.

Nutritional value: Calories: 253, Fat: 9g, Carbohydrates: 26g, Proteins: 17g, Sodium: 591mg, Phosphorus: 300mg, Potassium: 160mg.

7. Cheese and Asparagus Crepe Rolls with Parsley

 Serving: 1 crepe

 Preparation Time: 10 minutes

 Cooking Time: 15- 20 minutes

Ingredients:

- » 12 asparagus spears
- » 1 bundle of parsley
- » 2 ounces cream cheese
- » 1 egg, beaten
- » 1/4 cup of fresh cream
- » 1 teaspoon of lemon juice
- » 1/2 teaspoon black pepper
- » 1/3 cup all-purpose flour
- » 1/2 cup fresh water
- » 2 egg whites only
- » 4 tablespoons unsalted butter (or oil)

Directions:

- » Steam asparagus for 6 to 8 minutes.
- » Season with lemon juice, green cream sauce, puree cream cheese with parsley, and other seasonings. Salt and pepper can also be used according to taste. Set aside.

- » To create crepes, mix the egg, water, flour, egg white, and two tablespoons of melted butter until a smooth batter.
- » In a saucepan (8 to 10-inch crepes or sauté pan), melt 1/2 tablespoon butter. Pour in 1/3 cup crepe batter and flip the pan to evenly distribute the batter. Cook until the sauce is bubbling and the edges are beginning to brown. Cook for a few minutes on the opposite side. Place on a platter to cool. To create 4 crepes, repeat with the remaining butter and batter.
- » Spread cream cheese filling on crepes. At the end of each crepe, equally, distribute the asparagus stalks and tightly wrap them into rolls.
- » Refrigerate for one hour after wrapping in foil. Before serving, cut cooled crepes into 3-4 pieces using a sharp knife.

- » *Tip:* Fill the crepe with shrimp instead of asparagus for a higher Proteins entrée. Grated shrimp, sauté in olive oil, put it aside to cool, and then fold into crepes.

Nutrients per Serving: Calories: 305, Fat: 24g, Carbohydrates: 16g, Proteins: 34g, Sodium: 530mg, Phosphorus: 470mg, Potassium: 870mg

Renal-Friendly Desserts Options

Their inclusion on the menu helps us feel full after a meal and compensate for low blood sugar. In addition, the desire to enhance one's mood via sugar consumption may be a contributing element. Sweet foods stimulate the synthesis of the hormone "happy hormone" in our bodies. Your behaviors play an essential part in this as well. The majority of individuals enjoy desserts. Desserts are also permissible on a renal diet in the same way. Here are some desserts recipes that you may want to consider:

8. Blueberry Corn Cobbler

 Serving: 9

 Preparation Time: 10 minutes

 Cooking Time: 45 minutes

Ingredients:

» 1/3 cup (or 79 ml) of milk
» 1/4 teaspoon (or 1.25 g)of baking soda
» 1 egg. beaten
» 2 tablespoons (or 30g)of unsalted butter
» Half teaspoon (or 2.5g) of cream of tartar
» 5.5 ounces white corn flour
» 5.7 ounces of honey
» 2 pounds of blueberries

Directions:

» Preheat the oven to 375 degrees Fahrenheit (190 degrees Celsius).
» In a separate mixing bowl, whisk together the butter, milk, egg, cream of tartar, and baking soda.
» Stir in the corn flour and 1/2 cup honey until all lumps are gone.
» In a 9-inch baking dish, spread the blueberries to the bottom.
» Drizzle the leftover honey over the berries.
» Over the berries, drop the mixture by tablespoons.
» Bake for 30–35 minutes, or until the top is lightly browned and the berries have popped.

Nutrients per Serving: Calories: 216, Proteins: 2.9g, Carbohydrates: 45.5g, Fats: 2g, Sodium: 48.3mg, Phosphorus: 26.mg, Potassium 155mg

9. Proteins Booster Blueberry Muffins

 Servings: 12 muffins

 Preparation Time: 15 minutes

 Cooking Time: 40 minutes

Ingredients:

- Half cup butter softened
- 1 ¼ cups sugar
- 1 teaspoon vanilla extract
- ½ teaspoon of salt
- 2 eggs, beaten
- 2 teaspoons of baking powder or baking soda
- Half cup of milk
- 2 cups of blueberries, washed, drained and picked over
- 3 teaspoons of sugar
- 2 cups of flour

Directions:

- Preheat the oven to 375 degrees Fahrenheit.
- Lightly cream the butter and 1 1/4 cup sugar together.
- One at a time, add the eggs, beating thoroughly after each addition. Pour in the vanilla extract.
- Sift the flour, salt, and baking powder, then add the flour and milk to the combined mixture.
- 1/2 cup blueberries, crushed with a fork and folded into the batter. Combine the remaining whole berries in a mixing bowl.
- Fill a 12-cup standard muffin pan halfway with batter and bake for 20 minutes. Sprinkle the 3 tablespoons sugar on top of the muffins and bake for 30-35 minutes at 375 degrees.
- Remove the muffins from the pan and set them aside to cool for at least 30 min. Assuming you store the muffins uncovered, they will be overly wet the next day if they survive that long.

Nutrients per Serving: Calories: 250, Proteins: 3g, Carbohydrates: 30g, Fats: 3 g, Sodium: 100mg, Phosphorus: 73mg, Potassium: 54mg

10. Fresh Berry Fruit Salad with Yogurt Cream

 Servings: 8

 Preparation Time: 5 minutes

 Cooking Time: 20 minutes

Ingredients:

» 250 ml (or 1 cup) of blackberries
» 250 ml (or 1 cup) of raspberries
» 1 tablespoon of lemon juice, fresh
» 250 ml (or 1 cup) blueberries, fresh or frozen
» 250 ml (or 1 cup) red cherries, pitted and halved
» 30 ml (or 2 tablespoons) honey
» 500 ml (2 cups) yogurt
» 60 ml (or ¼ cup) honey

Directions:

» Combine the berries and honey in a mixing dish.
» Combine other Ingredients in a separate dish to make yogurt cream.
» Place a dollop of yogurt cream in the middle of each dish and top with a berry fruit salad.

Nutrients per Serving: Calories: 117, Proteins: 3.7g, Carbohydrates: 27g, Fats: 0.4g, Sodium: 16mg, Phosphorus: 30mg, Potassium 100mg.

11. Apple and Blueberry Crisp

 Servings: 8

 Preparation Time: 10 minutes

 Cooking Time: 55 minutes

Ingredients:

» 1 and 1/4 cups (or 310 ml) of quick-cooking rolled oats
» 6 tablespoons (or 90 ml) non-hydrogenated margarine, melted
» 1 tablespoon of lemon juice
» 1/4 cup (or 60 ml) of brown sugar
» 4 teaspoons of corn starch
» 1/4 cup (or 60 ml) of all-purpose flour
» Half cup (or 125 ml) of brown sugar
» 4 cups of blueberries, fresh or frozen
» 2 cups (or 500 ml) oof grated or chopped apples
» 1 tablespoon (or 15 ml) margarine, melted

Directions:

» Heat the oven to 350 degrees Fahrenheit with the center rack in place.
» Integrate the dry Ingredients: into a mixing bowl. Stir in the butter until the mixture is barely moistened. Put it aside.
» Blend the brown sugar and cornstarch in a 20cm square baking dish. Toss in the lemon juice and fruits. Bake for 55 minutes to 1 hour, or until golden brown, on top of the crisp mixture. Present warm or chilly.

Nutrients per Serving: Calories: 318, Proteins: 3.3g, Carbohydrates: 52g, Fats: 12g, Sodium: 148mg, Phosphorus: 93mg, Potassium: 180mg

12. Almond Meringue Cookies

 Servings: 24 cookies

 Preparation Time: 15 minutes

 Cooking Time: 40 minutes

Ingredients:

» 2 egg whites or 4 tablespoons of pasteurized egg whites (allow to come to room temperature)
» 1 teaspoon of cream of tartar
» Half teaspoon of almond extract
» Half teaspoon of vanilla extract
» Half cup of white sugar

Directions:

» Preheat the oven to 300 degrees Fahrenheit.
» Whisk Egg whites and cream of tartar together until quadrupled in volume. Beat in the remaining Ingredients until stiff peaks form.
» Push one teaspoon of meringue onto a parchment-lined baking sheet using the back of the other spoon, using two teaspoons.
» Bake for about 25 minutes at 300°F, or until meringues are crisp. Keep the container sealed if stored.

Nutrients per Serving: Calories: 37.9, Proteins: 0.6g, Carbohydrates: 9g, Sodium: 6mg, Phosphorus: 3mg, Potassium: 3mg

13. Raspberry Cheesecake Mousse

 Serving: 6

 Preparation Time: 5 minutes

 Cooking Time: 10 minutes

Ingredients:

» 1 cup of light whipped topping
» 1 teaspoon of finely grated lemon zest
» 1 teaspoon of vanilla extract
» 1 cup raspberries, fresh or frozen
» 18oz package cream cheese, room temperature

Directions:

» Mix cream cheese until frothy, then add 1 cup of Splenda granular and beat until melted. Combine the lemon juice and vanilla extract in a mixing bowl.
» Set aside a few raspberries to use as a garnish. C crush the remaining raspberries with a fork and mix Splenda granular in the remaining 14 cups until melted.
» Fold the light whipped topping into the cream cheese mixture, then fold the crushed raspberries softly but rapidly.
» Fill six serving glasses halfway with mousse and refrigerate until willing to serve.
» Before serving, garnish the mousse with fresh raspberries and a flower of fresh mint.

Nutrients per Serving: Calories: 257, Proteins: 10g, Carbohydrates: 29g, Fats: 15g, Sodium: 54mg, Phosphorus: 90mg, Potassium 128mg.

14. Cranberry Lemon Parfait

 Serving: 12

 Preparation Time: 5 minutes

 Cooking Time: 10 minutes

Ingredients:

» 1 store-bought food cake
» 2 eggs, beaten
» 2 cups of fresh water
» Half pound fresh cranberries
» 1 teaspoon of orange zest
» Half cup of white sugar
» 1 teaspoon of vanilla
» 1/3 cup of lemon juice
» ¾ cup white sugar
» 4 tablespoons of butter or margarine

Directions:

» For cranberry compote, in a saucepan, combine all of the Ingredients. Cook until the cranberries have broken down and the mixture has thickened. This dish may be served hot or chilled.
» Now for lemon curd, beat together eggs, lemon juice, zest, and sugar over a saucepan of boiling water until the mixture thickens.
» Remove the pan from the heat and stir in the chilled butter.
» In a parfait glass, layer angel food cake (store purchased) with cranberry compote and lemon curd to finish the dessert.
» Serve with fresh berries and mint as garnish.

Nutrients per Serving: Calories: 222, Proteins: 3g, Carbohydrates: 41g, Fats: 5.4g, Sodium: 63 mg, Phosphorus: 17mg, Potassium: 72mg.

Chap no. 5

Renal-Friendly Snacks

. . . .

Some individuals consume three meals each day. Some people consume six little meals each day. Others may find that one meal blends into the next. Whether you're a strict eater or a frequent "grazer," you're bound to have a Snack. You don't have to give up Snacks if you have chronic kidney disease (CKD), whether in the early stages, dialysis, or any other kidney problem. However, you'll need to prepare ahead of time to feel good about incorporating Snacks into your renal diet. On the renal diet, Snacking is OK as long as you select good choices. Rather than consuming high-Sodium foods like a small bag of potato chips, a piece of renal-friendly fruit is a better choice. It would be best to consider how much you consume regularly. Snacking does not have to be associated with a sense of guilt. Your renal dietician will explain the best Snack options if your doctor advises you to boost your calorie intake. When your hunger isn't as strong as it should be, Snacks may help make up for it.

15. Cranberry Dip with Fresh Fruit

 Servings: 24

 Preparation Time: 5 minutes

 Cooking Time: 10 minutes

Ingredients:

» 8 ounces of sour cream
» Half cup of whole berry cranberry sauce
» 4 pears, medium-sized
» 4 apples, medium-sized
» 1/4 teaspoon of nutmeg
» 1/4 teaspoon of ground ginger
» 4 cups of pineapple, fresh
» 1 teaspoon of lemon juice

Directions:

» In a food processor, combine the nutmeg, sour cream, ginger, and cranberry sauce until thoroughly combined. Place in a small bowl.
» Cut pineapples into bite-size chunks. Cut each apple and pear into 12 pieces. Toss them with lemon juice to keep apple and pear pieces from browning.
» Arrange fruit on a plate and place a dip bowl in the center. Refrigerate until ready to present.

Nutrients per Serving: Calories: 70, Proteins: 0g, Carbohydrates: 13g, Fat: 2g, Sodium: 8mg, Phosphorus: 15mg, Potassium 80mg.

16. Shrimp Spread with Crackers

 Serving: 8

 Preparation Time: 5 minutes

 Cooking Time: 15 minutes

Ingredients:

- » 1/4 cup of light cream cheese
- » 1 tablespoon of parsley
- » 2 and 1/2 ounces of shelled shrimp. cooked
- » 1 tablespoon of no-salt-added ketchup
- » 1 teaspoon of Worcestershire sauce
- » 1/4 teaspoon of hot sauce
- » Half teaspoon of herb seasoning blend
- » 24 matzo crackers, miniatures

Directions:

- » Allow cream cheese to soften in the refrigerator.
- » In a mixing bowl, mince the shrimp and add it to the hot sauce, herb seasoning, cream cheese, Worcestershire sauce, and ketchup
- » On each cracker, spread 1 teaspoon of the spread. Garnish with parsley, minced.

Nutrients per Serving: Calories: 57, Proteins: 3g, Carbohydrates: 7g, Fat: 1g, Sodium: 69mg, Phosphorus: 30mg, Potassium 28mg

17. Soft Ginger Cookies

 Servings: 24

 Preparation Time: 10 minutes

 Cooking Time: 20 minutes

Ingredients:

» 2 and 1/4 cups of all-purpose white flour
» 2 teaspoons of ground ginger
» 3/4 cup of butter, unsalted and at room temperature
» 1/4 cup of liquid low cholesterol egg substitute
» 1 teaspoon of baking soda
» 3/4 teaspoon of ground cinnamon
» 1/2 teaspoon of ground cloves
» 1-1/8 cups of sugar, granulated
» 1/4 cup of molasses

Nutrients per cookie: Calories: 142, Proteins: 2g, Carbohydrates: 20g, Fat: 6g, Sodium: 59mg, Phosphorus: 30mg. Potassium 22mg

Directions:

» Preheat the oven to 350 degrees Fahrenheit (180 degrees Celsius).
» Toss the ginger, cloves, flour, cinnamon, and baking soda in a medium mixing basin. Remove the item from circulation.
» For 30 seconds on medium speed, whip butter in a large mixing bowl using an electric mixer. 1 cup of sugar, whisked in.
» Combine the liquid egg replacement and the molasses in a mixing bowl.
» Whisk the flour, salt, and baking soda in a large mixing bowl.
» One 1/2-inch-thick dough "1 heaping spoonful of dough was used for each ball. To coat the balls, roll them in the leftover sugar.2-1/2" diameter balls "on a cookie sheet that hasn't been buttered
» Bake for 10 minutes, or until puffed and lightly golden. (Be careful not to overcook the potatoes.)
» Cool for 2 minutes on the cookie sheet before moving to a wire rack to cool completely.

18. Orange and Cinnamon Biscotti

 Servings: 2

 Preparation Time: 20 minutes

 Cooking Time: 1 hour 8 minutes

Ingredients:

- » ½ cup of butter, unsalted and at room temperature
- » 2 teaspoons of grated orange peel
- » 1 teaspoon of ground cinnamon
- » 1 teaspoon of vanilla extract
- » 2 cups of all-purpose flour
- » 1 teaspoon of cream of tartar
- » 1 cup of sugar
- » 2 large eggs, lightly beaten
- » Half teaspoon of baking soda
- » ¼ teaspoon of salt

Directions:

- » Spray 2 baking sheets with nonstick cooking spray.
- » Beat the sugar and unsalted butter in a large bowl until well mixed.
- » Add eggs one at a time, beating well after each addition.
- » Beat in orange peel and vanilla.
- » Mix cream of tartar, flour, salt, cinnamon and baking soda in a medium-size bowl.
- » Add dry Ingredients to the butter mixture and mix until incorporated.
- » Divide the dough in half. Place each half on a prepared sheet. With lightly floured hands, form each half into a log shape 3 inches wide by three-quarters of an inch high. Bake until dough logs is firm to the touch, about 35 minutes.
- » Remove the dough from the oven and allow it cool for 10 minutes.
- » Transfer dough to work surface. Using a knife, cut on a diagonal into ½-inch-thick slices. Arrange cut side down on baking sheets.
- » Bake until the bottom is golden, about 12 minutes.
- » Turn biscotti over; bake until bottoms are golden, about 12 minutes longer.
- » Transfer to a wire rack and cool before serving.

- » *Tip:* Refrigerate the dough for thirty minutes to form into logs more easily.

Nutrients per Serving: Calories: 149, Fat: 6g, Carbohydrates: 22g, Proteins: 14g, Sodium: 220mg, Phosphorus: 150mg, Potassium 90mg.

19. Homemade Herbed Biscuits

 Servings: 12

 Preparation Time: 10 minutes

 Cooking Time: 25 minutes

Ingredients:

» 1 and ¾ cups of all-purpose flour
» 1 teaspoon of cream of tartar
» 3 tablespoons of chives or any other herb, fresh or dry, to taste
» ¼ cup of mayonnaise
» Half a teaspoon of baking soda
» ⅔ Cup of skim milk
» Nonstick cooking spray

Directions:

» Preheat the oven to 400 degrees Fahrenheit. Spray a cookie pan with cooking spray after that.
» Combine flour, cream of tartar, and baking soda in a large mixing basin. Then, using a fork, stir in the mayonnaise until the evenly coated coarse cornmeal.
» Combine the milk and herbs in a separate dish and stir into the flour mixture. Stir until everything is well mixed.
» On a cookie sheet, drop generous teaspoons of the mixture. 10 minutes in the oven
» Keep it refrigerated until you're ready to use it.

Nutrients per biscuit: Calories: 109, Fat: 4g, Carbohydrates: 15g, Proteins: 3g, , Sodium: 88mg Phosphorus: 80mg, Potassium: 55mg

20. Chickpea and Avocado Salads

 Servings: 4

 Preparation Time: 15 minutes

 Cooking Time: 0 minutes

Ingredients:

» 2 avocados
» 7 ounces canned chickpeas
» 10 ounces cherry tomatoes
» 2 ounces arugula
» 1/2 red Tropea onion
» 15 black Greek olives
» 1 tablespoon lime juice (or lemon juice)
» 2 tablespoons extra virgin olive oil

Directions:

» Prepare the chickpeas: Drain and rinse them under running water.
» Cut the Ingredients. Dice the avocado, halve the cherry tomatoes, and thinly slice the red onion.
» Assemble the salad: In a large bowl, combine the chickpeas, avocado, cherry tomatoes, onion, and parsley.
» Prepare the vinaigrette: In a small bowl, mix the olive oil, lime juice, salt, and pepper.
» Dress the salad: Pour the vinaigrette over the salad and gently toss.
» Chill and serve: Let the salad rest in the refrigerator for at least 30 minutes before serving.

Nutrients per Serving: Calories: 250kcal, Fat: 20g, Sodium: 200mg, Carbohydrates: 40g, Proteins: 4g, Phosphorus: 75mg, Potassium 520mg.

21. Greek Yogurt Berry Parfait

 **Serving:** 2

 Preparation Time: 15 minutes

 Cooking Time: 0 minutes

Ingredients:

» 1 cup plain Greek yogurt (low-fat or non-fat)
» 1 cup mixed berries (such as blueberries, raspberries, or strawberries)
» 2 tablespoons chopped walnuts or almonds
» 1 teaspoon honey (optional, adjust to taste)
» Fresh mint leaves for garnish

Directions:

» In a glass or bowl, layer the Greek yogurt, mixed berries, and chopped nuts.
» Drizzle with a teaspoon of honey if desired.
» Garnish with fresh mint leaves.
» Serve chilled.

Nutrients per Serving: Calories: 150kcal, Fat: 6g, Sodium: 50mg, Carbohydrates: 15g, Proteins: 12g, Phosphorus: 155mg, Potassium: 200mg.

22. Baked Sweet Potato Chips

 Serving: 2

 Preparation Time: 2 minutes

 Cooking Time: 5 minutes

Ingredients:

» 2 medium sweet potatoes, washed and thinly sliced
» 1 tablespoon olive oil
» 1/2 teaspoon paprika
» 1/2 teaspoon garlic powder
» 1/2 teaspoon onion powder
» Salt to taste

Directions:

» Preheat the oven to 375°F .
» In a large bowl, toss the sweet potato slices with olive oil until evenly coated.
» Add paprika, garlic powder, onion powder, and salt to the bowl. Toss again until the sweet potato slices are evenly seasoned.
» Arrange the seasoned sweet potato slices in a single layer on a baking sheet lined with parchment paper.
» Bake in the preheated oven for 20-25 minutes, flipping the slices halfway through the cooking time, until the chips are crispy and golden brown.
» Once baked, remove the sweet potato chips from the oven and let them cool for a few minutes before serving.

Nutrients per Serving: Calories: 142, Fat: 4g, Sodium: 70mg, Carbohydrates: 17g, Proteins: 2g, Phosphorus: 60mg, Potassium 370mg.

Chapter no. 6

Salad Options

Salads can be eaten as Snacks as well as a full meal. Following are recipes of salads for renal diet:

23. Salad with Lemon Dressing

 Servings: 4

 Preparation Time: 10 minutes

 Cooking Time: 0 minutes

Ingredients:

» Heavy cream 1/4 cup
» Freshly squeezed lemon juice 1/4 cup
» Brown sugar 2 Tbsps.
» Chopped fresh dill 2 Tbsps.
» Finely chopped scallion 2 Tbsps. Green part only
» ground black pepper 1/4 tsp.
» English cucumber 1, sliced thin
» Shredded green cabbage 2 cups

Directions:

» Get a small bowl that combines the lemon juice, cream, sugar, dill, scallion, and pepper, and mix them well.
» Next, take a large bowl and combine the cucumber and cabbage.
» Place the salad in the refrigerator and chill for 1 hour.
» Mix well before serving.

Nutrition Facts per Serving:

Calories: 110 kcal, Fats: 6 g, , Proteins: 2 g, Carbohydrates: 13 g, Phosphorus: 10 mg, Sodium: 10 mg, Potassium: 70mg.

24. Chicken and Mandarin Salad

 Servings: 3

 Preparation Time: 40 minutes

 Cooking Time: 30 minutes

Ingredients:

- » ● 2 Chicken breast halves
- » ● 1/2 cup Celery
- » ● 1/2 cup Green pepper
- » ● 1/4 cup Onion, finely sliced
- » ● 1/4 cup Light mayonnaise
- » ● 1/2 tsp. Freshly ground pepper

Directions:

» Hurl chicken, celery, green pepper, and onion to blend. Include mayo and pepper. Blend delicately and serve.

Nutrients per Serving: Calories: 586.53 kcal, Fats: 57.9 g, Proteins: 30 g, Carbohydrates: 17.12 g, Phosphorus: 100 mg, Sodium: 160 mg, Potassium: 260mg.

25. Broccoli and Apple Salad

 Servings: 4

 Preparation Time: 15 minutes

 Cooking Time: 15 minutes

Ingredients:

- » ● 3 tablespoons low-Fats plain Greek yogurt
- » ● 2 tablespoons lite mayonnaise
- » ● 1 1/2 teaspoons of honey
- » ● 1 1/2 teaspoons apple cider vinegar
- » ● 1 cup fresh broccoli florets
- » ● 1/4 medium apple
- » ● 2 tablespoons diced red onion
- » ● 1 tablespoon fresh parsley
- » ● 2 tablespoons dried sweetened cranberries
- » ● 1 tablespoon walnuts

Directions:

- » Cut broccoli florets into bite-size pieces. Dice the 1/4 apple into small size pieces. Chop the parsley.
- » Whisk the yogurt, mayonnaise, vinegar, honey and parsley in a large bowl.
- » Add the remaining Ingredients into the bowl and coat it with the yogurt mixture.
- » Place In fridge to chill and let the flavors mix. Stir instantly before serving. (Optional)

Nutrients per Serving: Calories: 543.64 kcal, Fats: 42.88 g, Carbohydrates: 38.8 g, Proteins: 11.03 g, Sodium: 40.67 mg, Phosphorus: 170 mg, Potassium: 60mg.

26. Pasta Salad

 Servings: 4

 Preparation Time: 15 minutes

 Cooking Time: 15 minutes

Ingredients:

- » ● 1/4 tablespoon finely minced onions
- » ● 1/4 cup shredded carrots
- » ● 1/4 cup broccoli florets
- » ● 1/4 cup diced cucumber
- » ● 1/4 cup chopped red bell pepper
- » ● 2 tablespoons distilled white vinegar
- » ● 2 tablespoons olive oil
- » ● A pinch of garlic powders
- » ● A pinch of black pepper
- » ● 1/8 teaspoon dried oregano
- » ● 1/8 teaspoon celery seed
- » ● 2 ounces rotini pasta
- » ● 1 tablespoon grated Parmesan cheese
- » ● 1/4 teaspoon herb seasoning blend
- » ● A pinch of paprika

Directions:

- » Cut broccoli florets into small pieces. Set aside.
- » To make the dressing, combine vinegar, oregano, oil, pepper, garlic powder, celery seed, and onion. Set aside.
- » Cook pasta al dente.
- » Drain pasta, rinse, then toss with enough dressing to coat.
- » Add Parmesan cheese to pasta and refrigerate for at least 12 hours.
- » Add the remaining vegetables, herb seasoning blend, and paprika, and toss 2 hours before serving. Add more dressing if needed or desired.
- » Refrigerate until ready to serve.

Nutrients per Serving: Calories: 201.81 kcal, Fats: 14.44 g, Carbohydrates: 20.68 g, Proteins: 2.99 g, Sodium: 93.79 mg, Phosphorus: 74 mg

27. Roasted Red Pepper Hummus with Veggie Sticks

 Servings: 2

 Preparation Time: 15 minutes

 Cooking Time: 0 minutes

Ingredients:

» 1 cup canned chickpeas (rinsed and drained)
» 1 large roasted red bell pepper (store-bought or homemade)
» 2 cloves garlic, minced
» 2 tablespoons tahini (sesame seed paste)
» Juice of 1 lemon
» 1 tablespoon extra-virgin olive oil
» Salt and pepper to taste
» Assorted veggie sticks (carrot, celery, cucumber) for dipping

Directions:

» In a food processor, combine the chickpeas, roasted red pepper, minced garlic, tahini, lemon juice, and olive oil.
» Blend until smooth, adding a splash of water if needed to achieve the desired consistency.
» Season with salt and pepper to taste.
» Serve the roasted red pepper hummus with veggie sticks for dipping.

Nutrients per Serving: Calories: 160 kcal, Fats: 6g, Sodium: 200 mg, Carbohydrates: 27 g, Proteins: 7 g, Phosphorus: 100 mg, Potassium-250mg.

28. Turkey Salad

 Servings: 2

 Preparation Time: 15 minutes

 Cooking Time: 15 minutes

Ingredients:

» • 4 ounces cooked, unsalted turkey breast, cubed
» • 1 medium red apple, diced
» • 1/ 3 cup diced celery
» • 2 tablespoons + 2 teaspoons finely chopped onion
» • 1 tablespoon + 1 teaspoon mayonnaise
» • 2 teaspoons apple juice

Directions:

» Add all Ingredients into a medium bowl. Stir together until well mixed.
» Chill until ready to serve.

Nutrients per Serving: Calories: 748.28 kcal, Fats: 65.47 g, Carbohydrates: 29.26 g, Proteins: 12.78 g, Sodium: 120, Phosphorus: 100 mg, Potassium 189mg.

Vegetable Recipes

29. Glazed Snap Peas

 Servings:2

 Preparation Time: 10 minutes

 **Cooking Time:** 5 minutes

Ingredients:

» 1 cup snap peas
» 2 teaspoon Erythritol
» 1 teaspoon butter, melted
» ¾ teaspoon ground nutmeg
» ¼ teaspoon salt
» 1 cup of water for cooking

Directions:

» Pour water into the pan. Add snap peas and bring them to a boil.
» Boil the snap peas for 5 minutes over medium heat.
» Then drain water and chill the snap peas.
» Meanwhile, whisk together ground nutmeg, melted butter, salt, and Erythritol.
» Preheat the mixture in the microwave oven for 5 seconds.
» Pour the sweet butter liquid over the snap peas and shake them well.
» The side dish should be served only warm.

Nutrition Per Serving: Calories 64kcal, Fats 3.1mg, Carbohydrates: 7.1mg, Proteins: 2.8mg, Phosphorus: 110mg, Sodium: 75mg Potassium: 170mg

30. Vegetable Masala

 Preparation Time: 10 minutes

 Cooking Time: 18 minutes

 Servings: 4

Ingredients:

» 2 cups green beans, chopped
» 1 cup white mushroom, chopped
» 1 teaspoon minced garlic
» 1 teaspoon minced ginger
» 1 teaspoon chili flakes
» 1 tablespoon garam masala
» 1 tablespoon olive oil
» 1 teaspoon salt

Directions:

» Line the tray with parchment and preheat the oven to 360F.
» Place the green beans and mushrooms in the tray.
» Sprinkle the vegetables with minced garlic, ginger, chili flakes, garam masala, olive oil, and salt.
» Mix up well and transfer to the oven.
» Cook vegetable masala for 18 minutes.

Nutrients per Serving: Calories 81kcal, Fats 4.2mg, Carbohydrates 11.1mg, Proteins 1.9g, Phosphorus: 110mg, Sodium:75mg, Potassium: 280mg.

31. Cilantro Chili Burgers

 Servings: 3

 Preparation Time: 10 minutes

 Cooking Time: 15 minutes

Ingredients:

» 1 cup red cabbage
» 3 tablespoons almond flour
» 1 tablespoon cream cheese
» 1 oz scallions, chopped
» ½ teaspoon salt
» ½ teaspoon chili powder
» ½ cup fresh cilantro

Directions:

» Chop red cabbage roughly and transfer it to the blender.
» Add fresh cilantro and blend the mixture until very smooth.
» After this, transfer it into the bowl.
» Add cream cheese, scallions, salt, chili powder, and almond flour.
» Stir the mixture well.
» Make 3 big burgers from the cabbage mixture or 6 small burgers.
» Line the baking tray with baking paper.
» Place the burgers on the tray.
» Bake the cilantro burgers for 15 minutes at 360F.
» Flip the burgers onto another side after 8 minutes of cooking.

Nutrients per Serving: Calories: 227kcal, Fat: 18.6,Carbohydrates: 9.5mg, Proteins 9.9g Phosphorus: 116mg, Sodium: 95mg, Potassium: 200mg.

32. Jicama Noodles

 Servings:6

 Preparation Time: 15 minutes

 Cooking Time: 7 minutes

Ingredients:

» 1-pound jicama, peeled
» 2 tablespoons butter
» 1 teaspoon chili flakes
» 1 teaspoon salt
» ¾ cup of water

Directions:

» Spiralize jicama with the help of a spiralizer and place jicama spirals in the saucepan.
» Add butter, chili flakes, and salt.
» Then, add water and preheat the Ingredients: until the butter is melted.
» Mix it up well.
» Close the lid and cook noodles for 4 minutes over medium heat.
» Stir the jicama noodles well before transferring them to the serving plates.

Nutritients Per Serving:

Calories 182kcal, Fat 15.3mg, Carbohydrates 8.5mg, Proteins: 6.8g, Phosphorus: 110mg, Sodium: 75mg, Potassium 140mg.

33. Mushroom Tacos

Servings: 6

Preparation Time: 10 minutes

Cooking Time: 15 minutes

Ingredients:

- » collard green leaves
- » 2 cups mushrooms, chopped
- » 1 white onion, diced
- » 1 tablespoon Taco seasoning
- » 1 tablespoon coconut oil
- » ½ teaspoon salt
- » ¼ cup fresh parsley
- » 1 tablespoon mayonnaise

Directions:

- » Put the coconut oil in the skillet and melt it.
- » Add chopped mushrooms and diced onion. Mix up the Ingredients.
- » Close the lid and cook them for 10 minutes.
- » After this, sprinkle the vegetables with Taco seasoning and salt and add fresh parsley.
- » Mix up the mixture and cook for 5 minutes more.
- » Then add mayonnaise and stir well.
- » Chill the mushroom mixture a little.
- » Fill the collard green leaves with the mushroom mixture and fold them.

Nutrients per Serving: Calories 18kcal, Fats 0.8mg, Carbs 2.8mg, Proteins 0.9g Phosphorus: 150mg, Sodium: 75mg, Potassium: 250mg.

34. Minty Olives Salad

 Servings: 4

 Preparation Time: 10 minutes

 Cooking Time: 0 minutes

Ingredients::

- » 1 cup kalamata olives, pitted and sliced
- » 1 cup black olives, pitted and halved
- » 1 red onion, chopped
- » 2 tablespoons oregano, chopped
- » 1 tablespoon mint, chopped
- » 2 tablespoons balsamic vinegar
- » ¼ cup olive oil
- » 2 teaspoons Italian herbs, dried
- » A pinch of sea salt and black pepper

Directions::

- » In a salad bowl, mix the olives and the rest of the Ingredients, toss and serve cold.

Nutrients per Serving: Calories 240kcal, Fat: 8.2mg, Carbohydrates: 11.6mg, Proteins: 12mg, Phosphorus: 110mg, Sodium: 75mg, Potassium: 10mg.

35. Beans and Cucumber Salad

 Servings: 4

 Preparation Time: 10 minutes

 Cooking Time: 0 minutes

Ingredients:

» 10 ounces canned great northern beans, drained and rinsed
» 2 tablespoons olive oil
» ½ cup baby arugula
» 1 cup cucumber, sliced
» 1 tablespoon parsley, chopped
» A pinch of sea salt and black pepper
» 2 tablespoons balsamic vinegar

Directions:

» In a bowl, mix the beans with the cucumber and the rest of the Ingredients, toss and serve cold.

Nutrients per Serving: Calories: 190mg, Fat: 8.1mg, Carbohydrates: 11.6g, Proteins 4.6mg, Phosphorus: 110mg, Sodium: 75mg, Potassium: 200mg.

Chapter no. 8

Fish And Seafood Recipes

You can still enjoy seafood while on renal diet by following these recipes:

36. Baked sole with caramelized onion

 Servings: 4

 Preparation Time: 10 minutes

 Cooking Time: 20 minutes

Ingredients:

» 1 cup finely chopped onion
» ½ cup low-Sodium: vegetable broth
» 1 yellow summer squash, sliced
» 2 cups frozen broccoli florets
» 4 (3-ounce) fillets of sole
» Pinch salt
» 2 tablespoons olive oil
» Pinch baking soda
» 1 teaspoon dried basil leaves

Directions:

» Preheat the oven to 425°f.
» Add the onions. Cook for 1 minute; then, stirring constantly, cook for another 4 minutes.
» Remove the onions from the heat.
» Pour the broth into a baking sheet with a lip and arrange the squash and broccoli on the sheet in a single layer. Top the vegetables with the fish. Sprinkle the fish with salt and drizzle everything with olive oil.
» Bake the fish and the vegetables for 10 minutes.
» While the fish is baking, return the skillet with the onions to medium-high heat and stir in a pinch of baking soda.
» Transfer the onions to a plate.
» Top the fish evenly with the onions. Sprinkle with the basil.
» Return the fish to the oven; after this, bake it for 8 to10 minutes and serve the fish on the vegetables.

Nutrients per Serving: Calories: 188kcal, Fat: 6g, Sodium: 150mg, Phosphorus: 150mg, Carbohydrates: 12g, Proteins: 21g, Potassium: 600mg.

37. Thai tuna wraps

 Servings: 4

 Preparation Time: 10 minutes

 Cooking Time: 0-minute

Ingredients:

» ¼ cup unsalted peanut butter
» 2 tablespoons freshly squeezed lemon juice
» 1 teaspoon low-Sodium: soy sauce
» ½ teaspoon ground ginger
» ⅛ teaspoon cayenne pepper
» 1 (6-ounce) can no-salt-added or low-Sodium: chunk light tuna, drained
» 1 cup shredded red cabbage
» 2 scallions, white and green parts, chopped
» 1 cup grated carrots
» 8 butter lettuce leaves

Directions:

» In a medium bowl, stir together the peanut butter, lemon juice, soy sauce, ginger, and cayenne pepper until well combined.
» Stir in the tuna, cabbage, scallions, and carrots.
» Divide the tuna filling evenly between the butter lettuce leaves and serve.

Nutrients per Serving: Calories: 202kcal, Proteins: 16g, Fat : 11g, Carbohydrates: 10g, Sodium: 320mg, Phosphorus:331mg, Potassium: 150mg.

38. Grilled fish and vegetable packets

 Servings: 4

 Preparation Time: 15 minutes

 Cooking Time: 12 minutes

Ingredients:

» 1 (8-ounce) package of sliced mushrooms
» 1 leek, white and green parts, chopped
» 1 cup frozen corn
» 4 (4-ounce) Atlantic cod fillets
» Juice of 1 lemon
» 3 tablespoons olive oil

Directions:

» Prepare and preheat the grill to medium coals, and set a grill 6 inches from the coals.
» Tear off four 30-inch-long strips of heavy-duty aluminum foil.
» Arrange the mushrooms, leek, and corn in the center of each piece of foil and top with the fish.
» Drizzle the packet contents evenly with the lemon juice and olive oil.
» Bring the longer-length sides of the foil together at the top and, holding the edges together, fold them over twice and then fold in the width sides to form a sealed packet with room for the steam.
» Put the packets on the grill and grill for 10 to 12 minutes until the vegetables are tender-crisp and the fish flakes when tested with a fork. Be careful opening the packets because the escaping steam can be scalding.

Nutrients per Serving: Calories: 175kcal, Fat: 10g, Sodium: 98mg, Phosphorus:153mg; Carbohydrates: 8g, Proteins: 17g, Potassium: 400mg

39. Lemon butter salmon

. . . .

 Servings: 6

 Preparation Time: 15 minutes

 Cooking Time: 15 minutes

Ingredients:

» 1 tablespoon butter
» 2 tablespoons olive oil
» 1 tablespoon dijon mustard
» 1 tablespoon lemon juice
» 2 cloves garlic, crushed
» 1 teaspoon dried dill
» 1 teaspoon dried basil leaves
» 1 tablespoon capers
» 24-ounce salmon filet

Directions:

» Put all Ingredients except the salmon in a saucepan over medium heat.
» Bring to a boil and then simmer for 5 minutes.
» Preheat your grill.
» Create a packet using foil.
» Place the sauce and salmon inside.
» Seal the packet.
» Grill for 12 minutes.

Nutrients per Serving: Calories: 117kcal, Fat: 7.2g, Sodium: 180mg, Carbohydrates: 5.4g, Proteins: 8.1g, Phosphorus: 111 mg, Potassium: 400mg

40. Shrimp & broccoli

 Servings: 4

 Preparation Time: 10 minutes

 **Cooking Time:** 5 minutes

Ingredients:

» 1 tablespoon olive oil
» 1 clove of garlic, minced
» 1-pound shrimp
» 1/4 cup red bell pepper
» 1 cup broccoli florets, steamed
» 10-ounce cream cheese
» 1/2 teaspoon garlic powder
» 1/4 cup lemon juice
» 3/4 teaspoon ground peppercorns
» 1/4 cup half and half creamer

Directions:

» Pour the oil and cook garlic for 30 seconds.
» Add shrimp and cook for 2 minutes.
» Add the rest of the Ingredients.
» Mix well.
» Cook for 2 minutes.

Nutrients per Serving: Calories:383kcal, Proteins 24g, Carbohydrates: 46g, Fats: 11 g Sodium: 253 mg, Phosphorus: 266 mg, Potassium: 275 mg.

41. Shrimp in garlic sauce

 Preparation Time: 10 minutes

 Cooking Time: 6 minutes

 Servings: 4

Nutrients per

Ingredients:

» 3 tablespoons butter (unsalted)
» 1/4 cup onion, minced
» 3 cloves garlic, minced
» 1-pound shrimp, shelled and deveined
» 1/2 cup half and half creamer
» 1/4 cup white wine
» 2 tablespoons fresh basil
» Black pepper to taste

Directions:

» Add butter to a pan over medium-low heat.
» Let it melt.
» Add the onion and garlic.
» Cook it for 1-2 minutes.
» Add the shrimp and cook for 2 minutes.
» Transfer shrimp to a serving platter and set aside.
» Add the rest of the Ingredients.
» Simmer for 3 minutes.
» Pour sauce over the shrimp and serve.

Serving: Calories 469kcal, Proteins 28 g, Carbohydrates 28 g, Fats 28 g, Sodium: 300 mg, Phosphorus: 260 mg, Potassium: 260mg.

42. Fish taco

 Servings: 6

 Preparation Time: 40 minutes

 Cooking Time: 10 minutes

Ingredients:

- » 1 tablespoon lime juice
- » 1 tablespoon olive oil
- » 1 clove of garlic, minced
- » 1-pound cod fillets
- » 1/2 teaspoon ground cumin
- » 1/4 teaspoon black pepper
- » 1/2 teaspoon chili powder
- » 1/4 cup sour cream
- » 1/2 cup mayonnaise
- » 2 tablespoons nondairy milk
- » 1 cup cabbage, shredded
- » 1/2 cup onion, chopped
- » 1/2 bunch cilantro, chopped
- » 12 corn tortillas

Directions:

- » Drizzle lemon juice over the fish fillet.
- » Coat it with olive oil and then season with garlic, cumin, pepper and chili powder.
- » Let it sit for 30 minutes.
- » Broil fish for 10 minutes, flipping halfway through.
- » Flake the fish using a fork.
- » In a bowl, mix sour cream, milk and mayo.
- » Assemble tacos by filling each tortilla with mayo mixture, cabbage, onion, cilantro and fish flakes.

Nutrients per Serving: Calories: 482kcal, Proteins: 33 g, Carbohydrates: 46 g, Fats: 11g, Sodium: 70 mg, Phosphorus: 50 mg, Potassium: 33mg.

Renal-Friendly Meat Options

People with impaired kidney function must follow a renal or kidney diet to reduce the quantity of waste in their blood. Food and drinks eaten are the sources of waste in the blood. A renal diet may improve kidney function and delay the onset of total kidney failure. The renal diet is frequently advised for individuals with end-stage or late-stage chronic kidney disease. The renal diet is defined by a decrease in Sodium, potassium, and phosphor in the diet. Certain limits are in place to avoid accumulating these micronutrients in the bloodstream and minimize problems, including hypertension, fluid overload, arrhythmia, ortho diseases, and vascular calcifications. Following are recipes where you can eat meat and still carry on a renal diet:

43. Pork loins with leeks

 Servings: 2

 Preparation Time: 10 minutes

 Cooking Time: 35 minutes

Ingredients:

- » 1 sliced leek
- » 1 tablespoon mustard seeds
- » 6-ounce pork tenderloin
- » 1 tablespoon cumin seeds
- » 1 tablespoon dry mustard
- » 1 tablespoon extra-virgin oil

Directions:

- » Preheat the broiler to medium-high heat.
- » In a dry skillet, heat mustard and cumin seeds until they start to pop (3-5 minutes).
- » Grind seeds using a pestle and mortar or blender, then mix in the dry mustard.
- » Coat the pork on both sides with the mustard blend and add to a baking tray to broil for 25-30 minutes or until cooked through. Turn once halfway through.
- » Remove and place to one side.
- » Heat the oil in a pan on medium heat and add the leeks for 5-6 minutes or until soft.
- » Serve the pork tenderloin on a bed of leeks, and enjoy.

Nutrients per Serving: Calories: 306, Fats: 20g, Carbohydrates:10g, Phosphorus: 269mg, Sodium: 86mg, Proteins 23g, Potassium; 450mg.

44. Chinese beef wraps
. . . .

 Servings: 2

 Preparation Time: 10 minutes

 Cooking Time: 30 minutes

Ingredients:

» 2 iceberg lettuce leaves
» ½ diced cucumber
» 1 teaspoon canola oil
» 5-ounce lean ground beef
» 1 teaspoon ground ginger
» 1 tablespoon chili flakes
» 1 minced garlic clove
» 1 tablespoon rice wine vinegar

Directions:

» Mix the ground meat with garlic, rice wine vinegar, chili flakes and ginger in a bowl.
» Heat oil in a skillet over medium heat.
» Add the beef to the pan and cook for 20-25 minutes or until cooked.
» Serve beef mixture with diced cucumber in each lettuce wrap and fold.

Nutrients per Serving: Calories: 139kcal, Fat:5g, Carbohydrates: 2g, Phosphorus: 278mg, Sodium: 150mg, Proteins 18g, Potassium: 250mg.

45. Grilled skirt steak

 Servings: 4

 Preparation Time: 15 minutes

 Cooking Time: 8-9 minutes

Ingredients:

» 2 teaspoons fresh ginger herb, grated finely
» 2 teaspoons fresh lime zest, grated finely
» ¼ cup coconut sugar
» 2 teaspoons fish sauce
» 2 tablespoons fresh lime juice
» ½ cup coconut milk
» 1-pound beef skirt steak, trimmed and cut into 4-inch slices lengthwise
» Salt, to taste

Directions:

» In a sizable sealable bag, mix all Ingredients except steak and salt.
» Add steak and coat with marinade generously.
» Seal the bag and refrigerate to marinate for about 4-12 hours.
» Preheat the grill to high heat. Grease the grill grate.
» Remove the steak from the refrigerator and discard the marinade.
» With a paper towel, dry the steak and sprinkle with salt evenly.
» Cook the steak for approximately 3½ minutes.
» Flip the medial side and cook for around 2½-5 minutes or till the desired doneness.
» Remove from grill pan and keep side for approximately 5 minutes before slicing.
» With a clear, crisp knife, cut into desired slices and serve.

Nutrients per Serving: Calories: 156kcal, Fats: 2g, Carbohydrates: 4g, Phosphorus: 150 mg Sodium:250 mg, Proteins 14g, Potassium: 200mg

46. Roast beef

 Preparation Time: 25 minutes

 Cooking Time: 55 minutes

 Servings: 1

Nutrients per

Ingredients:

» 100gr Quality rump or sirloin tip roast

Direction:

» Place in roasting pan on a shallow rack
» Season with pepper and herbs
» Insert a meat thermometer in the center or thickest part of the roast
» Roast to the desired degree of doneness
» After removing from over for about 15 minutes, let it chill
» In the end, the roast should be moister than well done.

Serving: Calories: 393, Fat: 12g, Carbohydrates: 10g, Proteins: 36g Sodium:70g, Phosphorus:200mg, Potassium: 100mg.

47. Beef brochettes

 Servings: 1

 Preparation Time: 20 minutes

 Cooking Time: 1 hour

Ingredients:

- » 1 sliced large onion
- » 2 pounds thick steak
- » 1 sliced medium bell pepper
- » 1 bay leaf
- » ¼ cup vegetable oil
- » ½ cup lemon juice
- » 2 crushed garlic cloves

Directions:

- » Cut beef square blocks and place them in a plastic bag
- » Mix marinade Ingredients in a small bowl
- » Mix and pour over beef cubes
- » Seal the bag and chill for 3 to 5 hours
- » Divide Ingredients: onion, beef cube, green pepper, pineapple
- » Grill for about 9 minutes for each side

Nutrients per Serving: Calories 158kcal, Proteins: 24 g, Fats 6g, Carbohydrates 0g, Phosphorus: 30 mg, Sodium: 10 mg, Potassium: 460mg

48. Country fried steak

 Servings: 3

 Preparation Time: 10 minutes

 Cooking Time: 1 hour and 40 minutes

Ingredients:

» 1 large onion
» ½ cup flour
» 3 tablespoons. Vegetable oil
» ¼ teaspoon pepper
» 1½ pounds round steak
» ½ teaspoon paprika

Directions:

» Trim excess Fats from steak
» Cut into small pieces
» Combine flour, paprika and pepper and mix
» Preheat skillet with oil
» Cook steak on both sides
» When the color of the steak is brown, remove it to a platter
» Add water (150 ml) and stir around the skillet
» Return browned steak to skillet; if necessary, add water again so that the bottom side of steak does not stick

Nutrients per Serving: Calories: 304kcal, Proteins: 35 g, Fats: 15 g, Carbohydrates: 11 g, Phosphorus: 70 mg, Sodium: 30 mg, Potassium: 200mg.

49. Beef pot roast

 Servings: 3

 Preparation Time: 20 minutes

Cooking Time: 1 hour

Ingredients:

» Round bone roast
» 2 - 4 pounds chuck roast

Direction:

» Trim off excess Fats
» Place a tablespoon of oil in a large skillet and heat to medium
» Roll pot roast in flour and brown on all sides in a hot skillet
» After the meat gets a brown color, reduce heat to low
» Season with pepper and herbs and add ½ cup of water
» Cook slowly for 1½ hours or until it looks ready

Nutrients per Serving: Calories: 248kcal, Proteins:30g, Fat: 10 g, Carbohydrates: 5 g, Phosphorus: 190 mg, Sodium: 60 mg

50. Homemade burgers

 Servings: 2

 Preparation Time: 10 minutes

 Cooking Time: 20 minutes

Ingredients:

» 4 ounces lean 100% ground beef
» 1 teaspoon black pepper
» 1 garlic clove, minced
» 1 teaspoon olive oil
» 1/4 cup onion, finely diced
» 1 tablespoon balsamic vinegar
» 1/2ounce brie cheese, crumbled
» 1 teaspoon mustard

Directions:

» Season ground beef with pepper and then mix in minced garlic.
» Form burger shapes with the ground beef using the palms of your hands.
» Heat a skillet on medium to high heat, and then add the oil.
» Sauté the onions for 5-10 minutes until browned.
» Then add the balsamic vinegar and sauté for another 5 minutes.
» Remove and set aside.
» Add the burgers to the pan and heat on the same heat for 5-6 minutes before flipping and heating for 5-6 minutes until cooked through.
» Spread the mustard onto each burger.
» Crumble the brie cheese over each burger and serve!
» Try with a crunchy side salad!

» *Tip:* if using fresh beef and not defrosted, prepare double the Ingredients and freeze burgers in plastic wrap (after cooling) for up to 1 month.
» Thoroughly defrost before heating through completely in the oven to serve.

Nutrients per Serving: Calories: 157kcal, Proteins: 24g, Fat 13g, Carbohydrates: 0g, Phosphorus: 204 mg, Sodium: 150 mg, Potassium; 130mg.

51. Peppercorn Pork Chops

 Servings: 4

 Preparation Time: 30 min

 Cooking Time: 30 minutes

Ingredients:

» 1 tablespoon crushed black peppercorns
» pork loin chops
» 2 tablespoons olive oil
» 1/4 cup butter
» garlic cloves
» 1 cup green and red bell peppers
» 1/2 cup pineapple juice

Directions:

» Sprinkle and press peppercorns into both sides of pork chops.
» Heat oil, butter and garlic cloves in a large skillet over medium heat, stirring frequently.
» Add pork chops and cook uncovered for 5–6 minutes.
» Dice the bell peppers. Add the bell peppers and pineapple juice to the pork chops.
» Cover and simmer for another 5–6 minutes or until pork is thoroughly cooked.

Nutrition: Calories 317, Fat 25.7g, Sodium: 126mg, Carbohydrates 9.2g, Proteins 13.2g, Phosphorus: 115 mg, Potassium: 250mg.

52. Pork Chops with Apples, Onions

 Servings: 4

 Preparation Time: 30 min

 Cooking Time: 60 minutes

Ingredients:

» pork chops
» salt and pepper to taste
» 2 onions, sliced into rings
» 2 apples - peeled, cored, and sliced into rings
» tablespoons honey
» 2 teaspoons freshly ground black pepper

Directions:

» Preheat the oven to 375 degrees F.
» Season pork chops with salt and pepper to taste, and arrange in a medium oven-safe skillet. Top pork chops with onions and apples. Sprinkle with honey. Season with 2 teaspoons of pepper.
» Cover and bake for 1 hour in the preheated oven; pork chops have reached an internal temperature of 145 degrees F.

Nutrition: Calories 307, Fat 16.1g, Sodium: 100mg, Carbohydrates 26.8g, Proteins 15.1g, Phosphorus: 200 mg, Potassium: 250mg.

53. Baked Lamb Chops

 Servings: 4

 Preparation Time: 10 min

 Cooking Time: 45 minutes

Ingredients:

- » 2 eggs
- » 2 teaspoons Worcestershire sauce
- » 8 (5.5 ounces) lamb chops
- » 2 cups graham crackers

Directions:

- » Preheat the oven to 375 degrees F.
- » Mix the eggs and Worcestershire sauce in a medium bowl; stir well. Dip each lamb chop in the sauce and lightly dredge in the graham crackers. Then arrange them in a 9x13-inch baking dish.
- » Bake at 375 degrees F for 20 minutes, turn chops over and cook for 20 more minutes or to the desired doneness.

Nutrition: Calories176, Fat 5.7g, Sodium: 150mg, Carbohydrates 21.9g, Proteins 9.1g, Phosphorus: 100 mg, Potassium: 150mg.

54. Grilled Lamb Chops with Pineapple

 Servings: 4

 Preparation Time: 15 min

 Cooking Time: 55 minutes

Ingredients:

» 1 lemon, zest and juiced
» 2 tablespoons chopped fresh oregano
» 2 cloves garlic, minced
» black pepper to taste
» 8 (3 ounces) lamb chops
» 1/2 cup fresh unsweetened pineapple juice
» 1 cup pineapples

Directions:

» Whisk together the lemon zest and juice, oregano, garlic, salt, and black pepper in a bowl; pour into a resealable plastic bag. Add the lamb chops, coat with the marinade, squeeze out excess air, and seal the bag.
» Set aside to marinate.
» Preheat an outdoor grill for medium-high heat, and lightly oil the grate.
» Bring the pineapple juice into a small saucepan over high heat.
» Reduce heat to medium-low and continue simmering until the liquid has reduced to half its original volume, about 45 minutes.
» Stir in the pineapples and set aside.
» Remove the lamb from the marinade and shake off excess.
» Discard the remaining marinade.
» Cook the chops on the preheated grill until they start to firm and are reddish-pink and juicy in the center, about 4 minutes per side for medium rare. Serve the chops drizzled with pineapple reduction.

Nutrition: Calories 69, Fat 1.6g, Sodium: 45mg, Carbohydrates 8.5g, Proteins 5.9g, Phosphorus: 65 mg, Potassium: 200

Meal Plan

Sun		
Mon		
Tue		
Wed		
Thu		
Fri		
Sat		

28 Days Meal Plan

DAY 1

Breakfast

» 1 serving of chocolate Smoothie, with 1 tablespoon peanut butter, either mixed in or separate
» 1 slice 100% whole wheat bread with 1 tablespoon goat cheese and Coffee with up to 8 ounces of nonfat milk

Lunch

» 1 serving of Glazed snap peas
» 1/2 cup cherry tomatoes
» 1/2 cup baby carrots
» 1 medium apple

Snack

» 8 ounces nonfat plain yogurt
» 1 medium apple
» 10 almonds

Dinner

» 1 serving of baked eggplant slices
» 1 serving crack slaw
» 4 small roasted red potatoes

» 2 Healthy berry oatmeal muffins with apple and blueberry crisp

DAY 2

Breakfast

» 2 slices Toast with Almond Butter and Banana,
» 8 ounces nonfat milk or coffee with up to 8 ounces
» nonfat milk

Lunch

» 2 servings of Salad with vinaigrette
» 1/2 sliced avocado
» 10 almonds
» 1 medium peach

Snack

» 1 medium apple, sliced, with 1 tablespoons almond butter

Dinner

» 1 serving Stuffed Bell Pepper

- 1 cup steamed broccoli
- 1 serving Lemon Parfait

DAY 3

Breakfast

- 1 hard-boiled egg and 1 serving of Apples Oatmeal Custard
- 8 ounces nonfat milk

Lunch

- 1 serving Curried Chicken Salad Pita Sandwich
- 1 cup baby carrots and sliced bell peppers
- 1 cup of cherries

Snack

- 8 ounces nonfat plain yogurt
- 1 cup mixed berries
- 20 almonds

Dinner

- 2 servings of Roasted Butternut Squash Sou, topped with 1 tablespoon low-Fats yogurt
- 1 serving Brussels Sprouts Casserole
- 1 serving Chicken and Mandarin Salad
- 1 Delicious Orange and Cinnamon Biscotti

DAY 4

Breakfast

- 1 serving Quick and Easy Apple Oatmeal Custard

Lunch

- 1 serving Grilled Romaine Salad with 1 tablespoon
- 4 ounces baked boneless, skinless chicken breast
- 1/2 100% whole wheat pita bread
- 1 apple

Snack

- 1/2 cup nonfat cottage cheese with 1/2 cup sliced
- cucumbers and cherry tomatoes
- 1 medium orange

Dinner

- 1 serving Lemon Butter Salmon
- 1 cup baked sweet potato
- 1 cup steamed spinach

DAY 5

Breakfast

- 1 serving Tropical Smoothie
- 2 simply baked pancakes
- 2 tablespoons peanut butter or almond butter

Lunch

- 1 serving Italian Veggie Pita Sandwich, with 4ounces grilled or baked, roasted beef

» 8 ounces nonfat milk
» 1/2 cup grapes

Snack

» 1/4 cup hummus with sliced bell pepper and cucumber

Dinner

» 1 Homemade Burger
» 1 serving of beans and cucumber salad
» 1 cup of boiled brown rice and Zucchini Brownies

DAY 6

Breakfast

» 2 simple Pancakes
» 2 tablespoons real maple syrup
» Coffee with up to 8 ounces of nonfat milk
» 1/2 cup sliced strawberries

Lunch

» 1 serving of Turkey Salad with 1 1/2 cups spinach
» 1 medium kiwifruit

Snack

» 1 serving of Chocolate Smoothie

Dinner

» 1 serving Grilled Skirt Steak and 1/4 cup Grandma's Guacamole
» 1/2 cup Anna's Black Beans
» 1 cup Pear and Brie Salad

DAY 7

Breakfast

» 1 serving of Egg and sausage Breakfast sandwich
» 1 tablespoon almonds
» Coffee with 4 ounces of nonfat milk

Lunch

» 1 serving of Kale Vegetable Soup
» 8 ounces nonfat milk
» 1 toasted cheese sandwich with reduced-Fats mozzarella
» cheese on 1 slice of 100% whole wheat bread

Snack

» 2 to 3 addictive cookies
» 1/2 cup grapes

Dinner

» 2 slices of Mexican Pizza
» 1 serving pasta Salad
» 1 serving of saskatoon berry pudding

DAY 8

Breakfast

» 2 egg whites only
» Coffee with up to 8 ounces of nonfat milk
» 1 slice of 100% whole wheat bread
» 1/2 cup of grapes

Lunch

» 1 serving of Chicken and Mandarin Salad

- » 1/2 cup baby carrots
- » 1 medium peach

Snack

- » 20 almonds and a apple

Dinner

- » 1 serving of Cilantro chili burgers
- » Rice
- » 1 cup steamed spinach

DAY 9

Breakfast

- » Veggie Omelet
- » 1/2 cup mixed berries
- » Coffee with up to 8 ounces of nonfat milk

Lunch

- » 2 servings of Chicken Pasta Salad
- » 1 cup sliced carrot, bell pepper, and cucumber with
- » 2 tablespoons Basic Vinaigrette
- » 1 medium pear

Snack

- » 4 ounces nonfat cottage cheese
- » 1/4 cup of raw unsalted cashews
- » 1 medium sliced apple

Dinner

- » 1 serving of Chowmein
- » 1 serving of Grilled Asparagus
- » 1 cup of brown rice
- » 1 serving of Raspberry cheesecake mousse

DAY 10

Breakfast

- » 1 serving egg with smashed avocado toast
- » Coffee with up to 8 ounces of nonfat milk

Lunch

- » 1 serving pasta Salad,
- » 1 100% whole wheat pita bread
- » 1 medium peach

Snack

- » 1 serving of crunchy apple-maple Snack mix
- » baby carrots and sliced bell pepper

Dinner

- » 1 serving Baked Sunflower Seed–Crusted Turkey Cutlets
- » 1 serving of lime and chickpeas salad
- » 1 medium baked sweet potato
- » 1 tablespoon butter
- » 1 serving Minty olives Salad

DAY 11

Breakfast

- » 1 serving Wakeup Call! smoothie
- » 1 hard-boiled egg
- » 1 slice of 100% whole wheat toast

Lunch

- » 2 Beef Tacos
- » Barley blueberry salad
- » 1 medium orange

Snack

» 1 100% whole wheat English muffin with 2
» tablespoons peanut butter or almond butter
and 1 apple

Dinner

» 1 serving of beef pot roast
» 1 1/2 cups of white fish soup
» 1 cup boiled Brown Rice
» 1 cup of frozen grapes

DAY 12

Breakfast

» 1 hardboiled egg
» 2 cheese and asparagus Crepe rolls with parsley
» Coffee with up to 8 ounces of nonfat milk

Lunch

» 1 serving Roasted Butternut Squash Soup
» 1/2 cup sliced strawberries
» 1 cup baby carrots

Snack

» 8 ounces nonfat plain yogurt
» 1/2 cup blueberries
» 1/4 cup almonds

Dinner

» 2 Fish Tacos
» 1 sweet crustless quiche

DAY 13

Breakfast

» 2 Eggs
» 2 to 3 super simple baked pancake
» 1/2 grapefruit

Lunch

» thai tuna wraps
» 1 serving of salad with lemon dressing
» 2 corn tortillas
» 1 cup of grapes

Snack

» 1/4 cup raw unsalted nuts
» 1 apple

Dinner

» 1 serving of glazed snap peas
» 1 serving of turkey Salad
» 1 100% whole wheat pita bread
» 1 serving Berry corn Cobbler

DAY 14

Breakfast

» Coffee with up to 8 ounces of nonfat milk
» 1 slice 100% whole-wheat toast with 1 tablespoon of 100% fruit raspberry jam

Lunch

» 1 serving of curried fish cakes, topped with 1/2 sliced avocado
» 1/2 100% whole wheat pita bread
» 1 medium orange

Snack

» 1 medium sliced apple
» 2 tablespoons peanut butter

Dinner

» 1 serving of spiced lamb burgers, with 2 tablespoons shredded cheddar cheese. Small spinach salad with assorted veggies, like tomato, cucumber, carrot, bell pepper, and 2 tablespoons Basic
» Vinaigrette
» 1 serving Berry Sundae

DAY 15

Breakfast

» 2 slices Healthy French Toast
» 8 ounces nonfat milk

Lunch

» 1 serving of crack slaw
» 2 tablespoons baked eggplant sandwiches with 1 cup baby carrots
» 1 medium peach

Snack

» 1 apple
» 1/4 cup raw unsalted cashews

Dinner

» 1 serving of fish with mushroom
» 1 medium baked sweet potato
» 1 cup steamed spinach and 1 Brie-Stuffed Apple

DAY 16

Breakfast

» 1 serving Proteins Bowl
» 2 slices of 100% whole wheat toast with 2
» tablespoons 100% fruit jam Green tea

Lunch

» 1 serving Greek salad with 1 tablespoon of Lemon
» Vinaigrette, with 4 ounces grilled or baked
» 1 serving of beef brochettes
» 1 medium apple
» 20 almonds

Snack

» 8 ounces nonfat plain yogurt
» 1 cup mixed berries

Dinner

» 1 serving of Thai Curried Vegetables,
» with shrimp and broccoli
» 1 cup of brown rice
» 1 Banana

DAY 17

Breakfast

» 1 serving Green Avocado Smoothie
» Green tea
» 1/2 of bread
» 2 tablespoons of peanut butter

Lunch

» 1 baked trout

- » 1/2 cup Grandma's Guacamole
- » 1 cup baby carrots
- » 1 medium orange

Snack

- » 1/2 cup sliced strawberries
- » 1/2 cup sliced apple

Dinner

- » 1 serving of Lamb with prunes
- » 1 serving salad with 2 tablespoons Lemon dressing
- » Vinaigrette
- » 1/2 100% whole wheat pita bread
- » 1 serving Chocolate Smoothie

DAY 18

Breakfast

- » 1 serving Melon Mélange smoothie
- » 2 to 3 fluffy homemade buttermilk pancakes

Lunch

- » 1 serving of lemony lentil salad with salmon
- » 1 cup of grapes

Snack

- » 1 serving of dry-rubbed barbecue turkey wings
- » 1/2 cup baby carrots
- » 1/2 sliced medium apple

Dinner

- » 1 serving of jicama noodles

- » 1 medium mashed sweet potato with 1 teaspoon butter
- » 1 serving salad with 1 tablespoon of Lemon dressing
- » 1 cup mixed berries

DAY 19

Breakfast

- » 1 serving of turkey Breakfast burritos
- » 8 ounces nonfat milk or coffee with up to 8 ounces
- » nonfat milk
- » 1 cup mixed berries

Lunch

- » 1 serving of Salad with 1 tablespoon of Basic vinaigrette
- » 1 medium apple

Snack

- » 1 cup of sweet popcorn balls with 1 teaspoon butter
- » 1 medium orange

Dinner

- » crab cake
- » 1 serving of shrimp and broccoli
- » 1 serving Chocolate Dessert Smoothie

DAY 20

Breakfast

» 2 to 3 fluffy homemade pancakes
» 8 ounces nonfat milk
» 1/2 grapefruit

Lunch

» 1 serving of Salad with 1 tablespoon of Basic Vinaigrette
» baked trout
» 1 cup of grapes

Snack

» 2 sweet and nutty protein bars
» 2 tablespoons hazelnuts

Dinner

» 2 serving chowmein
» grilled or baked boneless, skinless chicken breast
» 2 servings of Salad with 2 tablespoons of Lemon dressing

DAY 21

Breakfast

» 1 serving chocolate Smoothie and quick and easy apple oatmeal custard
» Coffee with up to 8 ounces of nonfat milk

Lunch

» lemon and thyme lamb chops
» salad with 2 tablespoons of Vinaigrette
» 1 medium peach

Snack

» 1 medium apple with 2 tablespoons peanut butter

Dinner

» 2 to 3 mushroom tacos
» 1 serving Grilled Sweet Potato Steak Fries
» 3/4 cup of Strawberries with Whipped Cream

DAY 22

Breakfast

» 2 slices 100% whole wheat bread
» 2 ounces goat cheese

Lunch

» 1 serving Tuna Salad, with 1 ½ cups spinach
» 1/2 sliced avocado
» 1/2 cup cherry tomatoes
» 1 cup mixed berries

Snack

» 2 crispy cauliflower phyllo cups

Dinner

» 1 serving Vegetable masala
» 1 cup of brown rice
» 1/2 cup strawberries with 1 tablespoon home-made Whipped Cream

DAY 23

Breakfast

» 1 tablespoon sliced almonds and 2 to 3 sim-

ple pancakes
» Coffee with 8 ounces of nonfat milk or tea

Lunch

» 1 thai tuna wraps
» 1 medium orange

Snack

» 2 heavenly deviled eggs
» 1/2 cup grapes

Dinner

» 1 cup of white fish soup
» 1 serving of country fried steak
» 2 slices Pineapple

DAY 24

Breakfast

» 1 serving of tofu Breakfast scramble
» 1/2 grapefruit
» Green tea

Lunch

» A small salad with 1 cup of mixed greens, cherry tomatoes, and sliced cucumber
» 1 medium orange and beef croquettes

Snack

» orange and cinnamon biscotti with 1 cup of carrots and sliced bell pepper

Dinner

» 1 serving of baked sole with caramelized onion

» 6 small roasted red potatoes
» 1 small apple with 1 tablespoon chocolate

DAY 25

Breakfast

» 1 egg and sausage Breakfast sandwiches
» 8 ounces nonfat milk

Lunch

» 1 serving farro salad, with 4 ounces
» grilled or baked boneless, skinless chicken breast
» 1 medium orange

Snack

» 1 serving of shrimp spread with crackers
» 1 cup grapes

Dinner

» 2 mushroom tacos
» 1 serving salad with 1 tablespoon of Vinaigrette

DAY 26

Breakfast

» 1 hardboiled egg
» 1/2 grapefruit
» Coffee with 4 ounces nonfat milk, or green tea with lemon

Lunch

» 1 serving of baked eggplant slices with minty

olives salad

Snack

» 8 ounces nonfat plain Greek yogurt with ½ cup of blueberries

Dinner

» 1 serving of roast beef
» 1 slice of 100% whole wheat bread
» 2 slices of fresh pineapple
» 6–8 ounces of sparkling water

DAY 27

Breakfast

» 1 serving of chocolate Smoothie
» 1 egg and sausage Breakfast sandwiches

Lunch

» 1/2 cup black beans and 2 tablespoons cheddar cheese, 1/2 sliced avocado
» Salad with 2 tablespoons Basic Vinaigrette

Snack

» 20 hazelnuts
» 8 ounces nonfat plain yogurt
» 1/2 cup sliced strawberries

Dinner

» 1 serving of turkey salad
» 1 serving of grilled fish and vegetable packets
» 1 medium baked sweet potato
» 1 serving Berry Cobbler (1/2 cup blueberries)

DAY 28

Breakfast

» loaded veggie eggs
» 2 tablespoons peanut butter

Lunch

» 1 serving of chow mein
» 8 ounces nonfat milk
» 1 medium orange

Snack

» 1 cup cherries
» 20 almonds

Dinner

» 1 serving of Pasta Salad
» 1 serving of homemade burger
» 1 cup of frozen grapes

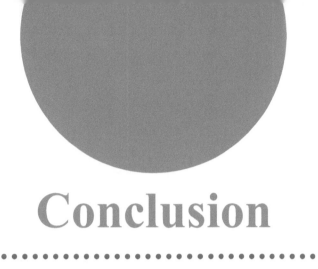

Conclusion

●●●●●●●●●●●●●●●●●●●●●●●●●●●●●●●

A person may prevent or reduce some health problems linked with chronic kidney disease by eating the right meals and avoiding foods high in salt, potassium, and phosphorus. The renal diet is the greatest option since it maintains kidney function while delaying the progression of total kidney failure. A renal diet stresses the need to eat high-quality protein and limit liquid consumption. The nutritious nature of keto acid supplemented, and the renal diet can have a cardiac preventive role in patients with chronic renal disease by affecting traditional and non-traditional cardiovascular risk when combined with dietary deception such as phosphorus, protein, and sodium restriction. Decreasing salt, potassium, and phosphorus consumption may help control blood pressure, which is important for lowering serum cholesterol and improving plasma lipid profiles. Low protein and phosphorus consumption are critical for avoiding and treating proteinuria and preventing and treating hypophosphatemia and secondary hyperparathyroidism, which are the primary causes of vascular calcification, heart diseases, and uremic mortality.

Leaving aside the previously contested effect on renal disease progression, proper nutritional treatment or a kidney-friendly diet, such as the renal diet, may help decrease the risk of cardiovascular disease in people with renal disease early on. According to this book, patients with reduced renal function should choose foods and diet plans cautiously. Finally, the healthiest diet for renal diseases and other health problems is the one that a person follows to establish and sustain a healthy lifestyle; thus, the renal diet is a powerful and effective method for dealing with critical renal diseases like CKD while remaining healthy and enjoying your favorite foods.

The kidney-friendly foods above are great options for those on a renal diet. Always with your healthcare professional about your dietary choices to guarantee that you implement the optimal diet for your specific requirements. Dietary limitations differ based on the kind and severity of kidney disease and the medical procedures used, such as medicines or dialysis. While adhering to a renal diet may seem restricted at points, many tasty items can be included in a healthy, nutritious, well-balanced, renal-friendly diet plan.

Recipes Index

» Almond Meringue Cookies   32

» Apple and Blueberry Crisp   31

» Baked Lamb Chops   78

» Baked sole with caramelized onion   60

» Baked Sweet Potato Chips   43

» Beans and Cucumber Salad   58

» Beef brochettes   72

» Beef pot roast   74

» Blueberry Corn Cobbler   28

» Broccoli and Apple Salad   47

» Cheese and Asparagus Crepe Rolls with Parsley   26

» Chicken and Mandarin Salad   46

» chickpea and avocado salads   41

» Chinese beef wraps   69

» Cilantro Chili Burgers   54

» Country fried steak   73

» Cranberry Dip with Fresh Fruit   36

» Cranberry Lemon Parfait   34

» Egg and Sausage Breakfast Sandwich   25

» Fish taco   66

» Fluffy Homemade Buttermilk Pancakes   20

» Fresh Berry Fruit Salad with Yogurt Cream   30

» Glazed Snap Peas   52

» Greek Yogurt Berry Parfait   42

» Grilled fish and vegetable packets   62

» Grilled Lamb Chops with Pineapple   79

» Grilled skirt steak   70

» Homemade burgers   75

» Homemade Herbed Biscuits   40

» Jicama Noodles   55

» Lemon butter salmon   63

» Loaded Veggie Eggs   23

» Minty Olives Salad   57

» Mushroom Tacos   56

» Oatmeal with Honey and Fruit   22

» Orange and Cinnamon Biscotti   39

» Pasta Salad   48

» Peppercorn Pork Chops   76

» Pork Chops with Apples, Onions   77

» Pork loins with leeks   68

» Proteins Booster Blueberry Muffins   29

» Raspberry Cheesecake Mousse   33

» Roast beef   71

» Roasted Red Pepper Hummus with Veggie Sticks   49

» Salad with Lemon Dressing   45

» Shrimp & broccoli   64

» Shrimp in garlic sauce   65

» Shrimp Spread with Crackers   37

» Soft Ginger Cookies   38

» Stuffed Breakfast Biscuits   21

» Super Simple Baked Pancake   24

» Thai tuna wraps   61

» Turkey Salad   50

» Vegetable Masala   53

Made in United States
Troutdale, OR
06/20/2024

20694358R00053